Twayne's United States Authors Series

Sylvia E. Bowman, *Editor*

INDIANA UNIVERSITY

Nathaniel P. Willis

NATHANIEL P. WILLIS

By CORTLAND P. AUSER

 132

Twayne Publishers, Inc.   ::   New York

To Doris, The Most Patient

Preface

EDWARD F. HAYWOOD'S statement that Nathaniel P. Willis was among the first authors in the United States "to work that vein of society writing" known as "polite literature" is still valid today.[1] This study follows a recommendation made by Professor Kenneth L. Daughrity that "Willis deserves another opportunity to win a more permanent place with the well-informed general reader."[2] Various historians in the field of American letters have, in fact, granted Willis a place, but for different reasons. Professor Daughrity, after careful examination, praised Willis' early essays, sketches, and poems. Professor Charles Huguenin has recognized both the strong and the weak points of Willis' literary criticism. Fred Lewis Pattee has argued that Willis deserves recognition for early contributions to the development of short fiction. A twentieth-century magazine of the smart set, *Town and Country* (the lineal descender of Willis' *Home Journal*) devoted a centennial issue in 1946 to appropriate commemorative statements.

Any student of Willis must indeed be grateful for the early studies made by Professor Henry Beers in the last century and by Professors Daughrity and Huguenin in this one. Too often literary historians have discredited Willis with cursory references to his dandyism in dress and to what they considered his affectations in writing. They have perpetuated earlier partisan judgments. What was a partial, incomplete judgment has become by quotation cliché and caricature.

Willis was first a journalist, or more specifically, in Edgar Allan Poe's word, "a magazinist." As a periodical writer, he fitted Poe's definition of one who was "disposed to put the greatest amount of thought in the smallest compass and disperse it with the utmost attainable rapidity." Poe's statement regarding Willis' versatility is also still valid for it calls him "a paragraphist, an essayist . . . a 'sketcher,' a tale-writer, and a poet."[3]

This study considers the entire scope and nature of Willis' various accomplishments and attempts a critical evaluation of his achievements.

In Chapter I, I examine the main events of Willis' early life which show his preparation for journalism. His achievements as a foreign correspondent for a periodical in his writing *Pencillings by the Way* receive attention in Chapter II. This and the next chapter also focus on his editorship of various New York journals. The remaining chapters, with the exception of the last, deal topically with the kinds of writing for which Willis was known. Thus, Chapters IV and V are concerned with his fictional work; Chapter VI, with his verses and plays. Chapter VII deals with his editorial work for the *Home Journal* and his society reporting. Finally, Chapter VIII covers later non-fictional travel works and miscellanies published in the 1850's. Chapter IX attempts an estimate of his contribution to American letters.

It should be remembered that Willis' work as a correspondent sending non-political prose copy back to the United States, as a purveyor of "culture," as an arbiter of taste, as a poetaster, an anthologist, and a playwright—all these roles are inextricably related to his journalistic career. At the same time that he employed certain eighteenth-century stylistic prose techniques, he was also a harbinger of styles to be used by twentieth-century magazinists.

Oliver Wendell Holmes observed that Willis "was something between a remembrance of Count D'Orsay and an anticipation of Oscar Wilde."[4] This typically Holmesian statement has a strong element of truth when one considers the public image which Willis consciously wished to project. Unless Holmes's judgment about appearances is qualified, an injustice is done Willis and his accomplishments. As a reporter of the events of the *beaumonde*, Willis was purposefully interested in fashion and taste. After an examination of his urbane essays, his more successful stories, and his travel sketches, one might modify Holmes's observation by stating that Willis' work, spanning as it does the forty-year period before the Civil War, recalls the tone and substance of essays by Irving's Geoffrey Crayon and at the same time looks ahead to themes and the locales of the stories of Henry James.

Lastly, in anticipation of the analysis of his life and work, I should certainly note that Willis was a vocal propagandist for the literary profession. If at times he erred in his campaigns, he may be forgiven in the light of what he accomplished. He did successfully acquire "status" for the profession of letters in America, and he ably edited periodicals which provided for the printing of the increasing number of literary productions of the times.

The present study, then, may to a degree restore Willis a few of the laurels of which Professor Arthur Hobson Quinn, echoing Professor Pattee, feels he has been "unjustly deprived."[5]

The author is especially grateful for the assistance given him by Professor Charles L. Huguenin who was an earlier reseacher of Willis' life and writings. Special thanks are owed to the entire library staff of the Air Force Academy. Under the supervision and guidance of Dr. George V. Fagan, staff members, particularly Mrs. Betty Fogler, were untiring in their efforts to render all possible assistance in securing material essential for this book through the co-operation of the Inter-Library Loan Service and affiliated libraries. Furthermore, thanks are due to Dr. Joseph Berthelot (of the Air Force Academy) for his continuing criticism and encouragement during research and composition.

CORTLAND P. AUSER

Bronx Community College
of The City University of New York

Contents

Chapter

Chronology   13

1. The Rise of "Natty" P. Willis, Magazinist   19

2. Penciller by the Way and Roving Correspondent   34

3. Knickerbocker Journalist and *Bon Vivant*   53

4. Teller of Tales   66

5. Sketcher of Society   90

6. Versatile Littérateur   108

7. Knickerbocker Spectator and Home Journalist   125

8. Chronicler and Critic of the Times   135

9. "The Profession of Taste"   146

Notes and References   150

Selected Bibliography   165

Index   171

Chronology

1806   Nathaniel Parker Willis born January 20 in Portland, Maine.

1812   The Willis family moves to Boston, Massachusetts.

1816   Nathaniel's father founds the *Boston Recorder,* a religious newspaper.

c.1820 Willis attends the Boston Latin School.

1821-   Attends Andover to prepare for his entrance into Yale
1822   University.

1823   Enters Yale in September; poem printed in *Recorder.*

1824-   Miscellaneous poems printed in *Recorder* and in other
1825   periodicals.

1827   Travels in New York, New England, and Canada during summer. Serves as Yale class valedictorian poet and is graduated in September. *Sketches* (poems) published in Boston.

1828   Editor of *Legendary,* published by Samuel Goodrich.

1829   Editor of the *Token,* an annual; begins publication of the *American Monthly Magazine* in April as its editor; publishes *Fugitive Poetry* in September.

1831   Ends publication of the *American Monthly Magazine* after the July issue; reads "Commencement Poem" at Brown University in September; leaves Boston to join editorial staff of the *New York Mirror* during summer. Sails for Europe as correspondent for *Mirror* in October; arrives at Havre, France, on November 3.

1832   Travels in France and Italy; visits in Paris, Florence, Rome, and Naples.

1833   In June, joins cruise of Mediterranean aboard the *USS Constellation.* Visits the Near East and returns to Malta in December.

1834 Tours Italy and visits Walter Savage Landor in Fiesole in April. Begins writing for *Court Magazine* and other British periodicals after his arrival in England, November 1.

1835 *Pencillings by the Way* published; on October 1 marries Mary Stace.

1836 Disputes with Marryat in January; *Inklings of Adventure* published. Sails for America in May; visits Niagara and, later, Washington, D.C.

1837 *Bianca Visconti* produced at the Park Theater in August. *Melanie and Other Poems* published. Buys house at Glenmary, Pennsylvania.

1839 Co-edits the *Corsair* with W. O. Porter in March. On May 20, sails for England. *The Tent Pitch'd* published.

1840 *Loiterings of Travel* published; discontinues publication of *Corsair*, March; in April, returns to the United States to write for periodical *Brother Jonathan* and to help edit the *Dollar Magazine*.

1841 Writes for *Godey's* and *Graham's*.

1842 *New York Mirror* ceases publication; sells Glenmary.

1843 With former associate George Pope Morris establishes the *New Mirror; Poems of Passion* published.

1844 *Lectures on Fashion* published. With Morris establishes the *Weekly Mirror* and the *Evening Mirror;* hires Edgar Allan Poe for the staff.

1845 Writes for the *Gift*, an annual; *Dashes at Life* published; *Poems, Sacred, Passionate, and Humorous* published. Wife Mary dies in childbirth. Visits England and Germany during the summer.

1846 With Morris, starts the *National Press* (later changed to *Home Journal*). On October 1, marries Cornelia Grinnell. *Prose Works* published.

1848 With Morris, edits *The Prose and Poetry of Europe and America; Poems of Early and After Years* published; writes for the *Opal,* an annual.

1849   *Rural Letters* published. Writes letter defending Poe in the October 20 issue of the *Home Journal*.

1850   Purchases land near Cornwall-on-the-Hudson. Is attacked by Edwin Forrest in June. *Life Here and There* and *People I Have Met* published.

1851   *Hurrygraphs* published.

1852   Sails for Bermuda and the West Indies on health cruise.

1853   Moves to Idlewild, New York. *Summer Cruise in the Mediterranean* published.

1854   *Fun Jottings* published; *Famous Persona and Places* published.

1855   *Rag Bag* published.

1856   Full-length novel *Paul Fane* published.

1857   Visits Washington Irving at Sunnyside.

1859   *The Convalescent* published.

1860   Travels west through Ohio, Wisconsin, and Missouri with father-in-law.

1861   Visits Baltimore and Washington. Meets Mrs. Lincoln. Begins series of reports for the *Home Journal* about the Civil War.

1865-
1866   Spends summer at Idlewild.

1867   Dies on sixty-first birthday.

Nathaniel P. Willis

CHAPTER 1

The Rise of "Natty" P. Willis, Magazinist

I *Early Life*

L IKE two of his contemporaries, Edgar Allan Poe and George
Pope Morris, with whom he was later to be associated,
Nathaniel Parker Willis achieved his laurels in a city other
than his birthplace. Poe, a native Bostonian, won fame in Rich-
mond, Philadelphia, and New York; Morris, a Philadelphian,
rose to unprecedented success as a journalist in New York.
Willis was born in Portland, Maine, on January 20, 1806, about
a year before the birthday of another Maine man of letters,
Henry Wadsworth Longfellow. Boston, however, was to be the
city which provided Willis with experience and a reputation;
New York was later to give him the fame and the congenial
professional associations which he sought. Early in his adult
career, he refused completely to become a "proper Bostonian"
and became instead an errant Knickerbocker.

Although American magazine journalism was to come into
its own during the period coincident with Willis' extended
editorial career, Willis himself was the third generation in his
family to achieve notoriety as writer and editor. His grand-
father had owned Boston's *Independent Chronicle* and had also
established newspapers in western Virginia frontier towns in
the eighteenth century. Willis' father (who was destined to
outlive his son) had in his teens set and inked types. Later, he
had served as a journeyman-printer in Boston and, finally, in
September, 1803, had founded the *Eastern Argus* in Portland,
Maine.[1] This event, coupled with another circumstance, was to
be significant in the younger Willis' background: his father

turned to a religious career and, combining his talents as a clergyman with those of a practicing journalist, founded a religious newspaper.

Because the elder Willis' venture was not successful in Portland, he decided to move his family on to Boston. There he established in 1816 the *Boston Recorder*. Nine years later, at the time of his son's graduation from college, he founded a second journal—*Youth's Companion,* a magazine for children which was to continue publication into the twentieth century. These two influences, the journalistic and the religious, inevitably had an impact upon the young boy. The father encouraged his son's attempts at versification. Willis was pleased to see his verses in print—an event which strongly nurtured his interest in writing and made him confident of his abilities. The restrictions, however, placed upon him as a member of a rigid Calvinist household provided an atmosphere against which the boy would react when he was released from familial surroundings.

Among other circumstances that contributed to shaping the personality of the boy was the fact that he was not a member of one of Boston's first families. This social situation might explain another facet of his character—a continued preoccupation with wanting to be liked by all with whom he associated. Lack of social position led him to reflect upon the question of natural ability *vis-à-vis* inherited social station. Willis repeatedly worked this theme in his prose writings.

Because of his strong orthodox beliefs, the father decided that it would be best to send his son to Yale, then a Calvinist stronghold. After courses at the Boston Latin School, he was sent to Andover in 1821.[2] At Andover, it is not surprising that, in view of his religious upbringing and restricted social life, Willis became interested in social activities.[3] He did, however, participate actively in a religious revival at the preparatory school. It was at Andover, too, that he became intensely interested in literature. His three-fold experiences in piety, pleasurable reading, and miscellaneous pastimes extended into the years which immediately followed when he attended Yale.

The Yale years were very important in crystallizing the attitudes of the future *bon vivant* and littérateur. In New Haven, he indulged his penchant for literature, reportedly reading widely and often neglecting his other studies; but he continued also his versifying, which a sympathetic father still printed in the poets' corner of the *Boston Recorder*.[4] Happily for his father, Willis chose scriptural subjects, suitable for the *Recorder's* select and particular audience, signing these religious pieces with the pseudonym "Roy." Professor Daughrity has pointed out that this pen name identifies one of Willis' two literary personalities. The "Roy" poems reveal elements of his character which resemble the pious nature of his father. And the serious strain in Willis' later writing certainly derived in part from this side of his character. In the 1820's and 1830's, Willis used a second pen name "Cassius" for poems dealing with secular subjects. As "Cassius," he revealed the polish and the elegance of the littérateur.

A perceptive comment by Edgar Allan Poe about this phase of Willis' life is that Willis' "literary career . . . had been modified . . . in a very remarkable degree by his personal one."[5] When Willis had settled in Boston after graduation and had become an editor, he began a campaign to establish an image of himself as the excellently groomed socialite. Having finally decided upon the profession of letters as his life work, he acquired editorial experience between graduation in 1827 and his founding the *American Monthly Magazine* in 1829. During this period, he gave more time to prose writing, but he continued printing his verses in the periodical.

Willis' association with Samuel P. Goodrich, first as an editor of the *Legendary* and later of the *Token*, increased his knowledge of the nature of the literary marketplace. The *Legendary* was similar in purpose, scope, and composition to many other literary journals of the late 1820's. It anticipated very closely the *New York Mirror*, with which Willis was to become associated in 1831, containing a large number of tales, ballads, and romances for its readers. In editorials, Willis stressed the importance of publishing what was "illustrative of American history, scenery, and manners."[6] The impressions which he had jotted down on his post-college tour through New York State and Canada were reworked as sketches for the periodical, the most noteworthy of the group being "Leaves from a Colleger's Album."[7] In them Willis created for the first time a fictional companion for his narrator to provide humorous touches. Also included in this collection is his "Unwritten Philosophy" and "Unwritten Poetry."

During 1828, Willis edited the *Token*, a gift-book annual. He took pride in the original contributions he secured for publication:[8] the works of such contemporary favorites as Grenville Mellen, Lydia Sigourney, and John Neal. He included five of his poems. For "The Ruse," the one prose work which he included, he drew upon his collegiate experience for a short, humorous sketch.[9]

Representative selections from the *Token* substantiate the generalization about early nineteenth-century annuals and gift books that they were heavily loaded with the sentimentally romantic; Willis chose love lyrics and poems about death, nature, religious topics, and the "noble savage." As editor he shows that he was well aware of the tastes of the reading public.

II *Editor of* American Monthly Magazine

Having served what might be termed both a literary and editorial apprenticeship under Goodrich, Willis launched the *American Monthly Magazine* in April, 1829. He did not take his new editorial position lightly, for he wrote: "It is with great diffidence that we appear before the Public as the Editor of a Literary Magazine. Aside from the question of capacity, there is a responsibility attached to an undertaking of this character upon which we cannot look with indifference. We feel that the influence of any periodical, generally circulated, is an important thing. . . ."[10]

He also committed himself editorially to establishing a cultural periodical with "the most prominent of the literary and political magazines of England as our professed model. . . ."[11] He modeled the *American Monthly* after the style and format of Thomas Campbell's *New Monthly Magazine*.[12] Well aware of the obstacles to the publication in America of a literary journal, he knew that American periodicals had comparatively few literary readers; he estimated that the circulation of his monthly would be limited to a thousand or two; and he also anticipated that distribution would be difficult.[13] He contrasted the American milieu for writers with the English one: "The immense patronage of English periodicals enables them to pay liberally for this material."[14] He was concerned with this problem through the years, becoming one of the staunchest supporters of an international copyright.

Other statements in the prospectus are significant in the light of his later editorship and his writing career. He revealed his plan to criticize books, but he made the point that he would not indulge in attacks upon the personalities of authors: "Whatever difficulties we may find in making our Reviews racy or interesting, we shall never descend, either to the ungentlemanly seasoning of personal abuse, or allusions to private differences."[15] He also announced a policy to which he adhered throughout his active writing life: he asserted that, although his journal would report and discuss political topics, he would not express party opinions. His aim was twofold: to interest and to amuse his readers.

A statement made by Poe in *The Literati* is relevant to the change which Willis made editorially in the journal within the first year of publication. Poe observed that Willis very early in his career (and Poe was acquainted with the author's work at the time he was editor of the *American Monthly Magazine*) understood that in America "a mere man of letters must ever be a cipher, and endeavored, accordingly, to unite the *éclat* of the littérateur with that of the man of fashion or of society."[16]

While Willis' periodical started in a conventional enough manner, a change soon occurred in his approach to his readers. In the fifth number, he told of having been the subject of personal abuse from various weeklies.[17] Willis struck out against any expression of journalistic malice toward individuals. Personal abuse, he felt, sacrificed "dignity and well-bred propriety." At the end of the editorial, he expressed a desire to change his style from that normally practiced by editors: "We trust . . . that you will not repel our familiarity. We should like to be more nearly acquainted with you than the remove of the third person always allows. We would have you sit down with us monthly to our dish of chit-chat and criticism, and allow us license we should claim if your feet were indeed under our mahogany."[18] He wanted to take the reader behind the editorial scenes by his coming down from "stilts" and being "natural awhile."[19]

Conscious then of the need for a change, he sought—a century before the profession of "image making" came into being—to modify his literary *persona*. In so far as Willis made the most of his own penchant for wearing fashionable clothes and appearing nattily dressed, just so far is Poe's evaluation correct that his success was due to his "physical temperament."[20] This image, then, which he created in his editorial columns had its origins not only in his desire to exemplify himself as the epitome of the fashionable gentleman but also in his sense of humor and in his wish to be well known and successful in the field of belles-lettres. He found his stylistic model for witty editorial chatter in the *Noctes* of writer "Christopher North."

The image of dilettantism was developed through a number of columns. For his readers, Willis pictorially furnished the editorial room with exotic objects and inhabitants. To it he invited the imaginary reader to take his ease. In addition to an old mahogany desk, Willis described his leather-bottomed dormeuse, a Chinese cupid ink holder, a velvet butterfly ink wiper, and a vase of Hungary water. Nearby his two pet dogs Ugolino and L.E.L. made themselves comfortable in the wastepaper basket. On the desk were old volumes, while the new ones stood upright between a long-necked Rudesheimer and a "slender Curacoa." A South American trulian completed the collection. To this office came the editor's friend Tom Lascelles, a confidant, and Cousin Sybil, who listened attentively as Willis read from his favorite authors.[21] In a spirit of humor, he suggested that he had "exchanged peculiarity for popularity"[22] and indicated that he was no longer bound to be sentimental but was "determined to follow the spirit of the age, and be an anti-everything-we-used-to-be-editor."[23]

Willis admitted that he loved table gossip. He was delighted when he found this type of light chatter in the *Book of the Boudoir* by a Lady Morgan, recently published in England. She, he felt, had gotten into print something of the spirit of "pieces of dialogue, jeux d'esprit, passages of feeling and fun, happy trifles one would gladly rescue from oblivion":[24] "We love this rambling, familiar gossip. It is the undress of the mind. We would read grave and dignified authors, but we would do it as we perform the duties of life. There should be a time afterwards for things that are lighter. . . ."[25] Calling Lady Morgan's work a "scrapbook," he followed her pattern in the same issue by beginning a separate feature with this title. For the purposes of this informal, gossipy department, he created Cousin Sybil to whom he read his favorite selections from his own scrapbook. The following month another column of light banter appeared, "Tete-a-

Tete Confessions."[26] His approach may be sensed from his justification of the tangential: "Blessings on his head who first invented digression! How should we write—how should we talk—how should we spice an article, or avoid entanglements in a *tête-a-tête* . . . if it were not for this sweet privilege?"[27]

Willis made a few significant remarks in the form of advice to writers for magazines—statements anticipating Poe's observations on the requirements for brevity. In the March, 1830, issue of the *American Monthly* Willis recommended:

> Magazine writers should be brief and crisp—dashing *in medias res* at the first sentence. Sink rhetoric. Nobody cares how you came to think of your subject, or why you wrote upon it—of course, the *exordium* is unnecessary. Commence with your leading thought and avoid irrelevant digressions. You may be less scholastic, but you will be more original and ten times as amusing.
>
> Do not be too grave. It is one of the great faults of magazine writers. Periodical readers expect to be amused, and would exchange all the dignity of a Number for a witticism. Not that you should be flippant or funny—but you should write as if your heart was warm with humor, and good humor, and you could not bar gaiety out. Nothing is so stupid as a mere dissertation—without anecdote, without facts, without sprightliness or novelty or wit. Cultivate humor—quiet humor.[28]

Throughout his career, Willis usually followed closely the advice that he had offered. He did, however, aspire to write a long fictional work: and he repeatedly stated—as an excuse for not fulfilling his hope—that the only market in America at the time was for the short forms of writing.

The informal editorial pose which Willis assumed during his first year with the *American Monthly* may partially explain why Poe characterized him as being too "readily self-dispossessed."[29] There is certainly some evidence that the abusive remarks of a few editors about Willis did sting; but one should not, however, picture the young editor as so overly sensitive that these statements completely overwhelmed him. He regained his sense of humor after such temporary annoyances and had enough perspective to answer appropriately. When Buckingham of the *Courier* passed on to him an epigram making fun of his works "Unwritten Poetry" and "Unwritten Music,"

Willis parodied the parodist.[30] He indicated at another time that perhaps Buckingham had caused him to be slightly solemn, but "every man has his whimsies, and ours is to love dogs, birds, and abusive editors."[31]

The editorial pages of the *American Monthly Magazine* during the years of Willis' editing reveal much about his personality, his interests, his background, and his journalistic virtuosity. The subjects of his critical essays, his editorial comments, and the topics and the style of his sketches and stories—all suggest the paths that his talents were to take in the 1830's and 1840's. Many sections of the magazine reveal a man widely read and continually reading—one who was knowledgeable of works in contemporary American and British literature, one who was versed in British and Continental classics. Poe erred when he underestimated Willis' mental abilities, but even such a latter-day critic as Fred Lewis Pattee unfortunately followed Poe's dicta. Pattee stated that "the past did not appeal to him [Willis]; Scott and Irving did not touch him; he cared nothing for legends and little for books."[32] Pattee's erroneous conclusions may also have derived from generalizations made by detractors about Willis, but the simple facts reveal that he was a voracious reader. The critics in Willis' own time who objected to what seemed to them airy, affected passages in his writing failed to take into account the extent of his reading, his own perspicacious critical judgments, his often expressed love of many English and Continental writers, and his gentlemanly and sympathetic encouragement of younger writers.

Any reader will find that Willis referred to or quoted extensively from the works of many authors in his critical articles and editorials, and in a variety of other departments of the journal. He was obviously well acquainted with the works of Shakespeare and many of his contemporaries. At different times he mentioned Ford, Raleigh, Webster, Heywood, Marlowe, Beaumont, Sidney, and Jonson.[33] Jeremy Taylor, Browne, and Burton were among his favorites. He had comments upon the work of Dante, Cervantes, and Spenser. He admitted a distaste for Fielding, Swift, Pope, and Dryden; but he expressed his enthusiasm for Sterne, Defoe, MacPherson, Milton, Addison, Lamb, Southey, Coleridge, Wordsworth, Shelley, Byron, and Keats.[34]

Among the classical writers, he was interested in Virgil, Cicero, Horace, and Juvenal. Among contemporary British authors, he read Praed, Landor, Campbell, Scott, Disraeli, Rogers, Bulwer, Hemans, and Landon. Among the Americans, he praised Dana, Bryant, Irving, Cooper, Halleck, Sprague, Leggett, Paulding, and Sedgwick.[35] Matters related to the contemporary literary scene could be found in such articles as "Passages from After-noon Reading," "Present American Literature," "The Profession of Authorship," "Some Thoughts upon Works of Fiction," "National Literature," and in the review of Basil Hall's *Travels in North America in the Years 1827 and 1828.* [36]

Much of the writing shows the influence of many British authors in poetry and in prose. His travel letters from the Continent and from the British Isles reveal a firsthand acquaintance with the work of many of the literati whom he had the occasion to meet personally. Indications of the extent of his reading are also found in the miscellaneous feature articles which he either composed for the journal himself or reviewed in his position of editor before their publication in the *American Monthly*. For example, he recommended, as a good talisman against ennui or moodiness, the keeping of a personal scrap-book. He wrote of the great enjoyment which he continually derived from copying items from his own "choice reading":[37] ". . . a manuscript book of choice scraps, anecdotes, odd thoughts, queer bits of reading—things which we transcribed from old library books we thumbed in our boyhood, to read over over when the books themselves, and the years in which we read them, should be forgotten. We love to idle away an afternoon upon them—reading one and then musing, or, if a friend is by us, conversing upon it with a rambling disconnectedness."[38] Very often he reprinted an excerpt from his own scrapbook in "The Editor's Table," quoting extensively in one instance both from the work of Jeremy Taylor and from Burton.[39]

Willis' versatility showed by the variety of his own work printed in the journal. He published sketches of his travels and fictional adaptations of the material such as "Letters of Horace Fritz," "Notes upon a Ramble," and "Pencillings by the Way."[40] Short stories appeared in the periodical. Many of these—such as "Baron von Raffleoff," "Captain Thompson," and "The Fancy Ball"—were reprinted in other periodicals at later dates. A few, like "The Exile" and "The Last Bachelor," were never republished.[41] Almost monthly, he included one of his poems; and many of these popular verses such as "Saul," "The Scholar of Thebet Ben Chorat," "The Dying Alchymist," "The Belfrey Pigeon," and "The Wife's Appeal" reappeared in other periodicals in the 1830's and the 1840's.[42]

Very often he revealed within an extended editorial his skill as an essayist writing of topics of personal interest in the manner of Charles Lamb. For example, he showed his sensitivity to the change of season in an apostrophe to June:

> We know nothing of a more restless tendency than one of these fine, old fashioned, June days—one that begins with a morning damp with a fresh south wind, and gradually clears away in a thin white mist till the sun shines through at last, genial and luxurious, but not sultry, and everything looks clear and bright in the transparent atmosphere. We know nothing which seduces the very eye and spirit of a man, and stirs in him that gipsey longing, which, spite of disgrace and punishment made him a truant in his boyhood.[43]

On such a day, he concluded, even his own "precarious livelihood" faded into the shadow.[44]

Critical comments in issues of the monthly significantly provide additional insights into his tastes, as well as information about what standards he employed for literary judgment. Reviewing *Henry Neele's Literary Remains* in April, 1829, he criticized negatively what he identified as "boarding school poetry, and lack-a-daisical prettyisms."[45] He took this opportunity to level a charge at reviewers who he believed were often men of "impure taste," "reckless and extravagant."[46] In similar vein, he often found the annuals "flotillas of trash."[47]

With Bulwer-Lytton's *The Disowned* before him, Willis identified the author as belonging to "a new school of romance writers" or, more correctly, to a "department of a much larger literary school."[48] Perceptively, he wrote: "Fashions in literature arise either from the genius of the most distinguished authors, by the effect of example and imitation, or from the influence of public taste, the character of the reading public, the greater or less diffusion of literature, and indeed from the general state of the literary market, by the demands which these circumstances give rise to, for certain kinds and styles of composition."[49]

With the increase in the number of writers, Willis further observed, writing had become more of a trade: "... the effect of it is to make the author consider rather what he can be best paid for than what he can write best."[50] In evaluating this novel, he made comments that, in the light of his later writing career, indicate characterizations of his own productions. He classified the fictional work among "the novels of high life" which dealt with the "peculiar spirit, amusements and customs of fashionable life." He labelled it the "school of Almack's, Pelham and Vivian Gray."[51] Willis felt that the author of *The Disowned* was one "trained in writing," "well acquainted with English literature," "an observer of life, but rather upon the surface ... of that accommodating school called men of the world."[52]

Supplementing these remarks on Bulwer were other observations made in the article, "Some Thoughts upon Works of Fiction":

> Ours is especially the golden age of Fiction, and the glancing and Protean shapes in which it appears, baffle all powers of classification. Novels have become to us one of the necessaries of life; and the differing tastes of the reading world must be all gratified. . . . We have the historical romance, exhibiting past events and characters in a series of magic lantern views—the stern outlines of reality softened down. . . . We have our fashionable novels, so called, descriptive of the habits of gentlemen and ladies who live in the west end of London. . . .[53]

Although Willis did not complete his first full-length novel until 1856, he identified in this article on fiction two areas he was to treat in his stories.

One other article in the *American Monthly* is interesting because of its possible relationship to a later work by Edgar Allan Poe. In the August, 1829, issue, there appeared "The Science of Criticism Systematized, or, The Art of Reviewing Made Easy." The unsigned article was probably by Willis since it was written in his light style and contained viewpoints similar to those he had expressed in other articles. It anticipated the humorous approach which Poe later employed in his "How to Write a Blackwood Article." Both articles suggest that criticizing in a review can be done by use of the proper formulas. Willis began his article with a direct attack on contemporary critics: "Modern reviewing may be defined [as] the art of bringing forward, under patronage of the author we pretend to criticise, our own misty speculations in regard to some favorite or indifferent subject."[54]

During this first publication year, writers were also criticized for the length of material that they sent to editors. Having recommended both brevity and humor to aspiring authors, Willis advised:

> Take it for granted that your article, at the first draught, is four-fifths too long. Cutting down requires resolution—but you gain experience as well as improve your article, by every excision. For the mode of doing it—begin by crossing out all explanatory sentences. Leave nothing but simple propositions. Young writers always explain a thing to death. Erase next everything that you have stolen from the American Reader, Elegant Extracts, the Complete Letter Writer, and well-thumbed authorities in general—there is a chance of their not being thought original.[55]

As the first anniversary of the establishment of the *American Monthly* came round, Willis indulged in reminiscence. He expressed his delight that the periodical had survived: "We entered, in distressed times, with the ebb of a boyish reputation against us, and the wrecks of unlucky precedents around, upon an enterprise depending wholly on public favor. We have been over-praised and abused, chilled with the indolence of critics and d---d (dosed) [*sic*] with their faint encouragement."[56] After two years of publication, he bid a fresh welcome to the reader and made a significant announcement: "We have made some essential alterations in our own affairs—taking the publishment of our magazine into our own hands, and becoming, thus, Editor, Proprietor and Publisher in one."[57] He asserted anew that he would not give up the editorship, for he wrote: "We established it under depressing circumstances without funds, and with the croaking of a hundred Editors in our ears...."[58] At this same time he made the important announcement of his plan to go abroad to Europe for a year or two. He hoped, he said, to sketch for the magazine "*First Impressions of Europe.*"

In less than a year, however, the *American Monthly Magazine* ceased publication. Although he had eagerly taken on the additional responsibilities of publisher and proprietor, he was not a man with a business sense; and the costs of publishing the *American Monthly* contributed to an increasing debt. It was no wonder that, along with his writing and reviewing, he could not properly administer the business functions of the magazine—even if he had had the talent to do so.

But the financial reason was probably not the sole one for his determining to move from Boston. At a later date he explained that Boston did not provide a congenial atmosphere for his writing. He had antagonized other journalists and magazinists such as the *Courier* editor Joseph Buckingham, William Snelling, and Lydia Maria Child. All had been outspoken in their criticism of what they considered Willis' snobbish pretensions. Moreover, the church society to which he had early belonged had read him out of membership because of his theatergoing.[59]

III *The Move to New York*

A short time after the publication of the July issue of the *American Monthly Magazine*, Willis made his move to New York City, a place more suitable to his temperament and his talents. Professionally, he found a person sympathetic to his work in George Pope Morris of the *New York Mirror*, who had been its editor since 1823. Morris had recognized Willis' talent and had commented favorably upon it in the pages of the *Mirror*. The position of co-editor of that publication must have seemed attractive to Willis, particularly when the responsibilities were those of a literary editor and not of a business manager. The man and the moment were happily met when he joined the *Mirror* during the summer of 1831.

The *Mirror* had been in the journalistic arena for eight years by 1831. Washington Irving's fame and success in New York had resulted in a stimulation of a literary self-consciousness among writers and *bon vivants*. The *Mirror* had commenced publication when a literary tradition had begun to assume shape. By 1831, the weekly was well established, annually increasing its circulation.

The *Mirror* had already taken advantage of Irving's popularization of the literary travel essay. Its contributors sentimentalized about much of the region's past and romanticized in articles and stories the places in the city's environs with which they were acquainted.

Willis most surely found in Morris' earlier prospectuses (normally reprinted with slight variation annually) what he himself had desired for his Boston monthly: a happy combination of literary pieces written for instruction and agreeable amusement.[60] This aim, which Morris had restated on many occasions, echoed Addison's declared objective in the tenth issue of the *Spectator:* "I shall endeavor to enliven morality with wit and temper wit with morality." Through the judicious and tactful guidance of Morris, the *Mirror* had carefully avoided many major journalistic frays. Political neutrality, too, had in part accounted for its success.

Morris' personality provided the basis for Willis' association with him to be a happy one. Coming from an obscure and lowly background, Morris had as a boy and young man, like Willis, learned many phases of the printing and publication business. Morris, however, during the years had cultivated a business sense and, moreover, enjoyed the responsibilities of the commercial department of the journal. He had learned to avoid the type of failures experienced by his first associate and co-editor, Samuel Woodworth.

Through direct and indirect experiences, Morris and Willis had each learned that editors could not direct the publication of a magazine to one highly specialized group. To do so was simply not remunerative. Shortly after Willis had joined the staff, an editorial indicated that the character of the *Mirror* would "necessarily be miscellaneous, embracing a great variety of matters and subjects."[61] It was also announced that the journal would carry in a distinctly lighter vein many items of local interest and news. This approach was in the tradition of Irving's *Salmagundi* and Knickerbocker writings, and Willis was particularly adept in this genre.

Among other announced editorial aims which reaffirmed earlier statements, the *Mirror* indicated its plan for providing its subscribers with "topics for conversation, to bring readers up to date with news of the fashionable world and the events of the beau monde."[62] These columns were to include what Morris and Willis labeled "chit-chat."[63] They enlarged upon this plan when they asked contributing writers to deal with the "commonplace occurrences of society—the trivial follies of the everyday vices and virtues, or peculiarities passing immediately around us...."[64] There is no doubt that Willis was the prime mover behind this announcement. He had in critical reviews and editorials asserted his wish to write "gossipy" columns.

Willis always wrote and edited with a continuing awareness of the importance of the tastes of female readers. His success with Morris and with the *Mirror* was immediate because he and his co-editor felt that American readers were perpetually in search of something new. Contemporaneity and novelty were the criteria. He practiced what he had preached in the *American Monthly.*

Willis had announced earlier in 1831 his intention of making a two-year trip through Europe. When he joined the *Mirror,* Willis no doubt had mentioned his plans to Morris. Both sensed the popularity of sketches and essays which had appeared about England and the Continent, and they knew they had to satisfy reading tastes. Willis, then, in the summer of 1831 "pushed" the idea of having the *Mirror* send correspondents abroad to report upon events, persons, and places. Until 1831, no journalist who had gone to Europe had been paid solely by one periodical to send copy back to the States for publication. Morris finally agreed to such a sponsorship. Willis' ingenuity and writing talents made the idea not only succeed but secure a more than adequate monetary return to the *Mirror* for its slight investment.

CHAPTER 2

Penciller by the Way and Roving
Correspondent

I *Impressionistic Traveler*

WHEN Willis set foot aboard the ship *Pacific* in October, 1831, he was enthusiastic about the venture. One of the first letters sent back to the States after his arrival in Havre, France, on November 3 revealed that he felt that "the dream of . . . [his] lifetime [formulated earlier in 1831] was about to be realized."[1] He described his excitement in another way: "It is a common thing enough to go abroad, and it may seem idle and commonplace to be enthusiastic about it, but nothing is common, or a trifle to me."[2] Although he had as a young man already gained a wide reputation, little did Willis sense that the trip was to ticket him for a journey to far greater fame than that achieved by many of his journalist colleagues who remained in America during the 1830's.

Not many other Americans of his day had the peculiar combination of talents which accounted for Willis' foreign success. His abilities matched those which he himself had described for the ideal travel writer when he had reviewed Henry E. Dwight's *Travels in the North of Germany in the Years 1825 and 1826* for the *American Monthly*.[3] Because he had had a wide reading with a thorough knowledge of literature, he was prepared, as he himself had required, to appreciate the many places with literary associations on the Continent. He was also anxious to receive an entire spectrum of impressions, for he felt that travel reports should not be cold statistics.

The ideal traveler should be a man with a wide knowledge of the practical arts. It was in this element, perhaps, that Willis was most lacking; he did not command sufficient knowledge of various aspects of the American economy to make extensive comparisons in this area. As for being a connoisseur, certainly Willis had to a marked degree established himself as an arbiter of works of taste. The many travel sketches reproduced in the *American Monthly* had shown a keenness of observation as he toured the United States and Canada. In his conduct as an editor and as a *bon vivant*, he had continually revealed a sense of fairness, as well as gentlemanly qualities, in his association with the various representatives of different groups in society. According to his own frames of reference, then, he was prepared for the job before him.

He had already learned the lesson of writing material for the readers of periodicals which Poe was to call the "light artillery of the intellect." Willis was true to his own dictum (one that must have kept him on the *qui vive*) as he composed the letters to the *Mirror*—"Periodical readers expect to be amused." His earlier review of Dwight's *Travels* had indicated how a book of travels was to be written:

> The feeling toward the author of a personal narrative, is somewhat peculiar. Our feelings are interested for himself. We read his book as if we knew him and was [*sic*] listening to a friend's description.
>
> We are [as] interested for the favorable conclusion of an adventure as himself, and adopt his partialities and his aversions, both personal and local, with readiness and ardor.
>
> The author should not confine himself to things about him. He should give us the impressions they make upon himself. We are with him there, by the old ruin or in the mighty cathedral, and we would have him tell us his sensations and describe the influences that affect a stranger standing for the first time there.[4]

A reader takes pleasure in reading travels "not to store up a mass of foreign localities and dimensions" but to benefit from the author's descriptive imagination. Willis characterized description as successful when it had the qualities of vividness and the power of familiarizing a scene so that the reader would feel himself there and "experience all the natural sensations of surprise and strangeness."[5] "A book," Willis added, "without this quality gives us the same idea of a country that a skeleton does of the human figure, or a chalk outline of a landscape in June. A book *with* this quality in any perfection is as rare as it is delightful. . . ."[6]

Willis was delighted to go the generally untrodden way of the reporter of foreign scenes. He must have realized how challenging it would be to undertake the trip sustained only by the stipend which Morris provided, and he had a confidence in himself without which he would have hardly succeeded to the extent that he did. In addition to his wide writing experience, he had succeeded to a degree in his desire to participate in Society. He had made many friends during his New Haven collegiate days, he had friendships with people in certain segments of Boston society, and he had become acquainted with a few Knickerbocker litterateurs. Adventurous, alert to the visible and sensuous world, and aware of persons and personalities, he must have felt that his European assignment was a sure step toward becoming a member of the *beau monde* and an opportunity to report what he thought and felt about its members. He knew, then, what the subjects of his letters should be; he sensed how best he would report his experiences; he was aware of the extent of his talents. Lastly, he was keenly aware of the nature of his readers' curiosity about persons and places, and he planned to satisfy their inquisitiveness. His literary market was ready.

One of the best evaluative statements about the letters which he sent to the *Mirror* was made by the author himself in 1844 when he sat down to edit them for publication: "They were literally what they were styled—notes written on the road, and dispatched without a second perusal. . . ."[7] His was a determination to give pictures of "living society where . . . [it was] in very high perfection."[8] In the first letter of the series, he realized that his language might often seem exaggerated, and he felt that what he wrote was the "mere" skeleton, "a goldsmith's inventory of the reality." Willis, whom many had already tagged as being too affected and ultra-sophisticated, admitted to becoming "a mere child in wonder."[9]

Generally, he sustained throughout the entire series a chatty, interesting, and completely impressionistic style. He did not attempt to do more than record impressions vividly, revealing himself as continually enthusiastic in his prejudices regarding persons and places. Time and again he was able in swift strokes to give his readers the picture of an individual against a particular background, or to characterize a place by the striking impressions he chose to record. In his fourth letter, he restated his objective by identifying it as recording "impressions, not statistics."[10]

After his arrival in Paris, Willis was attached to the embassy staff of Mr. William Cabell Rives, the American ambassador in France.[11] As such, he was entitled to wear the uniform of the staff and had entrees to people and to places which would have been more difficult for him to see as a private citizen and author.

Paris did not disappoint him. He was delighted by its people and its museums. His observations included discussions of all facets of Parisian life such as an Académie Royale ball and a dinner with the editors of the *Revue Encyclopédique*. There was so much to be seen that he concluded that "Paris is a world for research. . . . One might live a life of novelty without crossing the barrier."[12] He experienced sharp reactions as he visited the gambling houses, or as he looked steadfastly at the people frequenting the Tuileries. "The gardens are like a constant fête. It is a holy day without design or disappointment. It is a masque where everyone plays his character unconsciously."[13]

He sometimes allowed the faintest note of nostalgia to creep into his writing, recalling the "inimitable grace" of a single New England elm in the passage just before the following reflections on the gardens at the Tuileries: "The garden of the Tuileries is an idle man's paradise. Magnificent as it is in extent, sculptures, and cultivation, we all know that statues may be too dumb, gravel walks too long and level, and trees and flowers and fountains a little too Platonic with any degree of beauty."[14]

Despite his strong desire to participate in social events and his delight in watching ladies in the gardens, he paused to wonder about the artificial elements of much of Parisian life. "Everything gets travestied in this artificial society. The general ambition seems to be to appear that which one is not."[15] In contrast to these emotions, he was strong in his expression of sympathy for the Polish exiles who filled Paris and was indignant at the municipal guardsmen who used sabers to disperse a Parisian mob.[16]

He was able to juxtapose in an unforgettable short picture the green beauty of a Parisian season and the deaths from the plague.[17] His description of a masked ball at the height of the plague inevitably recalls to a reader's mind the unreal atmosphere of a later allegorized account of a similar setting and situation in Poe's "Masque of the Red Death."

Individual celebrities made impressions, which he took care to set down. He could not easily forget the philanthropy of James Fenimore Cooper in his support of American artists in Paris. On the other hand, he was both frank and unflattering as he sketched the notorious Countess Guiciolli: "Her cheek bones are high, her forehead is badly shaped, and altogether, the frame of her features is decidedly ugly. She dresses in the worst taste, too, and yet with all this, and poetry and celebrity aside the Countess Guiciolli is both a lovely and a fascinating woman. . . ."[18] He also attempted to characterize national types, as he had individuals. He described, if a bit romantically, the American abroad: "It is the independent, self possessed bearing of a man unused to look upon anyone as his superior in rank, united to the inquisitive, sensitive, communicative expression which is the index to our national character."[19]

When Willis finally left Paris, he felt that he had been there long enough to know it "from its broad faubourgs to its obscurest *cul de sac.*"[20] He started his trip to Italy on April 16, 1832; his stay in France had been approximately six months long.[21]

II *Sketches of Scenes*

The trip through Italy and the Near East deepened his feeling about art and sensitized his sight. He had, of course, given evidence of this interest in the pages of the *American Monthly* when he had written about Continental painters. This further development of his penchant for art-viewing had begun in Paris, where he visited several museums and associated with American artists. For example, he had reported in his seventh letter that he was particularly struck by Veronese's "The Marriage Supper at Cana." He also spent time watching Samuel Morse copy a

Murillo.[22] "I never realized so forcibly," he said later, "the beauty of sunshine. Architecture particularly is nothing without it."[23] Experiences of this nature led him to ponder over scenes that he observed and carefully select the appropriate descriptive words of comparison in his letters. He was to recollect many details later, when he wrote other sketches and stories, and he incorporated them into these compositions to pictorialize locales for his readers. An artist was often to be one of the main characters in a story either as a narrator or as a participant in the plot. Experiences in museums provided him with a firsthand knowledge of art from the spectator's viewpoint. From this background, he continually selected as he wrote, composing similes which sprang from his knowledge of painting.

During the summer and the autumn of 1832 he spent the time in Italy traveling from Florence to visit other sites and returning to his lodgings which he shared part of the time with the American sculptor Greenough whom he had met in Paris. While in Florence, Willis actually tried to learn the art of sculpturing. Although he did not become an art student, he employed these experiences as material in his novel *Paul Fane* and in shorter pieces.

Shortly after his arrival in Florence, the feeling of awe overcame him: "I have seen but one or two things, yet have felt so unequal to the description that but for my promise I should never write a line about them. Really, to sit down and gaze into one of Titian's faces for an hour and then go away and dream of putting into language its color and expression seems to me little short of superlative madness. I only wonder at the divine faculty of sight."[24] Viewing the "Venus of the Medicis" was a high point of his stay in Florence; Titian's "Bella" in the Pitti impressed him deeply. He also had words of praise for Raphael as he viewed "St. Cecilia."[25] Even the place where he resided during the stay in Florence was the room from which Thomas Cole, the American artist, had made sketches.

Willis' growing awareness of the beauty of painting was also evident when he compared the scenery in the Romagna to the "tints of a Rosa painting."[26] In Rome, he visited the studio of the German sculptor Thorwaldsen.[27] He was impressed also by what he called the grand plan of the Italian churches. Although at times he was outspokenly critical of the ceremonies of the Roman church, he admitted his delight in "haunting" chapels and cathedrals.[28]

Willis finished his traveling in Italy in the spring of 1833, and he left Leghorn on June 3rd, as a guest aboard the American frigate *Constellation* on which he sailed up the Adriatic. After visits to Vienna and Trieste he continued his pilgrimage. Byron's works served as his Baedeker, and his letters were filled with references to Byron; quite naturally he quoted from *Childe Harolde's Pilgrimage*. He made other literary allusions as he approached the Greek islands: "This is the proper dreamland. The 'Isle of Calypso' folded in a drapery of blue lies behind, fading into the distance . . . which caught Byron's eye as he entered Greece . . . and the Ionian sea is rippling under our bow, breathing from every wave of Homer, and Sappho, and 'sad Penelope.' "[29] On the Island of Egina, he sought out Byron's famed "Maid of Athens" (the model for the poem of that name), Teresa Makri, only to find that she had been married to a prosaic Scotsman by the name of Black.[30]

The Grecian mainland affected him deeply as he visited Athens:

> We passed two or three hours wandering about among the broken columns, and gazing away to the main and distant isles, confessing the surpassing beauty of Greece. Yet have its mountains scarce a green spot, and its vales are treeless and uninhabited, and all that constitutes desolation is there, and strange as it may seem, you neither miss the verdure, nor the people. . . .
> The mountains lean down into the valleys, and the plains swell up into the mountains, and the islands rise from the sea, with a mixture of boldness and grace altogether peculiar. . . .[31]

Memorable, too, is the passage in which Willis invoked the spirit of the past as he stood on Demosthenes' rostrum. He envisioned the ancient Greek orator exhorting the crowds. He saw the "calm Aristides," the handsome Alcibiades, and wise Socrates gazing upon a pupil. "How easily," he concluded, "is this bare rock, whereon the eagle now alights unaffrighted, repeopled with the shadows of the past."[32]

The U.S. frigate *Constellation,* continuing its Mediterranean cruise, took him finally to the Levant. The Near East triggered his imagination. The importance of the voyage was best stated in a letter which he addressed to the *Mirror* readers from aboard ship: ". . . life has run in deep a current with me of late, that the absence of incident seems like water without wine. The agreeable stir of travel, the incomplete adventure, the change of costumes and scenery, the busy calls upon the curiosity and the imagination have become, in a manner very breath to me."[33]

The European travels and the visit to the Near East supplied Willis with a backdrop for his romantic short stories. Letters sent to the States described the castles along the Dardenelles, a picnic on the plains of Troy, glimpses of Turkish military life, and views of Constantinople itself:

> Yet the world contains nothing like Constantinople. If we could compel all our sense into one, and live by the pleasures of the eye, it were a paradise transcended. The Bosphorus—the superb, peculiar incomparable Bosphorus, the dream-like, fairy built seraglio, the sights within the city so richly strange, and the valleys and streams around it so exquisitely fair, the voluptuous softness of the dark eyes haunting your every step on shore, and the spirit-like swiftness and elegance of your darting caique upon the waters.[34]

This was heady copy for readers back in the States. The full romantic appeal was there. Just as Willis had been inspired by Byron, so was he to inspire the young Bayard Taylor to seek out the bizarre and the faraway romantic. From these Near Eastern experiences were also to come Willis' own stories "The Gypsy of Sardis" and parts of the "Widow by Brevet."

There were other unforgettable stops for Willis. After spending five weeks in Constantinople, he was delayed in getting passage on a ship out of Smyrna. He finally shipped aboard the brig *Metamora* in December, 1833.[35] The letter which he composed for the *Mirror* aboard this ship was lost in transmittal, but Willis later reconstructed it, in 1836.[36] He landed at Malta and then traveled north through Italy staying for a while at Fiesole where he visited Walter Savage Landor.

Again, as he traveled north to Switzerland, he recalled Byron during his visit to Lake Leman and to Chillon. In Italy, the Milan Cathedral appeared to him as an "Aladdin creation": "The filmy traceries of Gothic fretwork, the needle-like minarets, the hundreds of beautiful statues with which each is studded, the intricate, graceful, and bewildering architecture of every window and turret, and the frostlike frailness and delicacy of the whole mass, make an effect altogether upon the eye that must stand high on the list of new sensations."[37]

Perhaps one of the best illustrations of his talent to get visual impressions down on paper was contained in the same letter, as he noticed the effect of the sunlight:

The sun struggles through the immense windows of painted glass staining every pillar and carved cornice with the richest hues, and wherever the eye wanders it grows giddy with the wilderness of architecture. The people on their knees are like paintings in the strong artificial light, the checkered pavement seems trembling with a quivering radiance, the altar is far and indistinct, and the lamps burning over the tomb of San Carlo, shine out from the centre like gems glistening in the midst of some enchanted hall.[38]

Although he continued to write travel essays for the rest of his career, he never equaled in this genre the description in many of these "Pencillings by the Way."

III *Reporter of the British* Beau Monde

As Willis was successful in pictorializing his travels in Europe and the Near East, he was equally able to sketch the personalities and the spirit of the *beau monde* which he came to know well in England. Professor Robert Spiller in *The American in England* states that there had been other reporters of the places of England "...but it was left to Nathaniel Parker Willis to make her scintillating present a reality to American readers."[39]

After his arrival in England on June 1, 1834, he used the personal letters of introduction to Lady Blessington which Walter Savage Landor had given him. She adopted him as a protege, and secured him introductions to many of the literati of England. Willis' letters about his meeting the famous hostess and sponsor of littérateurs was as sharp in delineation as his comments about Countess Guiciolli:

In a long library lined alternately with splendidly bound books and mirrors, and with a deep window of the breadth of the room, opening upon Hyde Park, I found Lady Blessington alone. The picture to my eye as the door opened was a very lovely one. A woman of remarkable beauty half buried in a fauteuil of yellow satin, reading by a magnificent lamp, suspended from the arch ceiling; sofas, couches, ottomans, and busts arranged in rather a crowded sumptuousness through the room; enamel tables, covered with expensive and elegant trifles in every corner, and a delicate white hand relieved on the back of a book, to which the eye was attracted by the blaze of its diamond rings.[40]

The groups in attendance which Willis described constituted a true republic of letters, and he later envisioned them as an absolute requirement for the establishment of a truly proper social life in such a metropolis as New York. At the soirées that she held, Willis met Bulwer-Lytton, Disraeli, and Procter (Barry Cornwall), whose works he had reviewed in the *American Monthly*. Not only did he write sketches of the appearance of these authors, but he was able to catch their conversational tones as they gathered for an evening or an afternoon party.[41]

He visited Charles Lamb not too long before the essayist's death. He had long been an admirer of Lamb and had praised his work highly in the Boston periodical. Writing from England, Willis stated that he would rather have one hour with Lamb than see all the sights of London.[42]

A description of Tom Moore gives an idea of Willis' ability to portray: "His eyes still sparkle like a champaign [*sic*] bubble, though the invader has drawn his pencillings about the corners; and there is a kind of wintry red, of the tinge of an October leaf, that seems enamelled on his cheek, the eloquent record of the claret his wit has brightened."[43] He wrote of Disraeli:

I might as well attempt to gather up the foam of the sea as to convey an idea of the extraordinary language in which he clothes his *description*.

He talked like a race horse approaching the winning post, every muscle in action, and the utmost energy of expression flung out in every burst. It is a great pity he is not in Parliament.[44]

After London, Willis toured the North Country, visiting Edinburgh and reporting upon the beauty of the scenery at Gordon and Dalhousie Castles, describing his visits to Lord Jeffrey and Christopher North (whose *Noctes* he had imitated in the *Amer-*

ican Monthly and whose style he later attempted to emulate in the editorials of the *New Mirror*).

Although Willis was to contrast in a few of his short fictional pieces the natural nobility of the American Indian and the artificial aristocracy of the English gentry, he compared in a late letter in the series the English aristocrat with the Indian in a different vein: "I should say a North American Indian, in his more dignified phase, approached nearer to the manner of an English nobleman than any other person. The calm repose of person and feature, the self-possession under all circumstances, that incapability of surprise or dereglement, and that decision about the slightest circumstance, and the apparent certainty that he is acting comme il faut is equally 'gentlemanlike' and Indian like."[45]

During the publication of many of the "Pencillings," he had been criticized in both the British and American press for indiscretion in describing private scenes. Willis, believing that he was emulating such a writer as Washington Irving, stated his rationale for such compositions: "Their interest as sketches by an American of the society that most interests Americans, and the distance at which they are published, justify them, I would hope, from any charge of indelicacy."[46]

The letters that Willis sent to the *Mirror* were printed between February 13, 1832, and January 14, 1836. They were generally dispatched on a weekly basis; but, because of inevitable delays in transportation by ship, they normally appeared about two weeks apart. There were 139 in all. Although he identified them collectively as "Pencillings by the Way," he called them "First Impressions of Europe" for the column in the *Mirror*. He was well aware that the pressure under which he wrote them did not comprise the best circumstances for composition. "This writing," he stated, "and sending off unrevised is the worst thing in the world for one's reputation."[47] He did feel, however, that the surroundings were inspirational: "I feel every day that my mind is ripening and laying up material which I could get nowhere else."[48] So particularly impressed by England was he that he predicted he would return once he had met his obligations to Morris and the *Mirror*.

Beers once indicated that Willis' ability to sketch a scene, as he did so often in the "Pencillings," was not surpassed by

Hawthorne, nor later by Bayard Taylor or Henry James. Unlike Longfellow, Willis did not dwell at length upon the literary associations of places. Nor did he introduce political matters or comments upon commerce or industry.

During his British stay, Willis was lionized by many literary and social coteries, a situation which Professor Daughrity has indicated was the basis for Poe's "quiz on Willis" in his sketch "Lionizing."[49] He contributed to three British periodicals: the *Court Magazine*, the *Metropolitan* (edited by Marryat) and the *New Monthly*. It was for them that he wrote, or reconstructed, such sketches and short stories as "Love and Diplomacy," "The Madhouse of Palermo," "Incidents on the Hudson," "Tom Fane and I," "Pedlar Karl," and "Scenes of Fear." Nor did Willis cease his publication the following year, for there appeared "F. Smith," "Love in the Library," "The Gypsy of Sardis," "The Cherokee's Threat," "The Revenge of Signor Basil," and "Larks on Vacation."[50] For these, he received money from British publications, a source of income which helped sustain him during his stay in Great Britain. Many of these works were later reprinted in the *Mirror*.

The experiences which he had among the various social groups he employed later in his fictional works: such experiences as the close association with Lady Blessington and his friendship with a Mrs. Skinner who introduced him to such littérateurs as Praed.[51] He became acquainted with Jane Porter, the authoress of *Scottish Chiefs* and with Joanna Baillie. With the former he carried on an extensive correspondence which continued over many years. Among other literary notables to whom he was introduced were Samuel Rogers and Thomas Campbell.

It was through Mrs. Skinner that Willis met the woman who was to become his wife, Mary Stace. Before their marriage on October 1, 1835, Willis traveled through England visiting such historic places as Warwick Castle and Kenilworth.[52] After a fourteen-day Parisian honeymoon, he returned to England to prepare both *Pencillings* and *Inklings of Adventure* for the press.[53] On March 31, 1835, Willis had published his *Melanie and Other Poems*. *Pencillings* was finally published in November of the same year. In March, 1836, *Inklings* appeared, containing many of the stories that he had contributed to British magazines.

IV *Stormy Petrel*

Although the popularity of Willis' letters assured an increase in the circulation of the *New York Mirror,* his reputation as a stormy petrel also widened his reputation in America. Morris underwent a series of minor crises in situations involving his roaming correspondent. Among other difficulties was the displeasure of members of the Catholic Church over the manner in which Willis had made statements about church ceremonies in Rome; another article incurred the wrath of an extremist Protestant organization; a third resulted in strong attacks from American journals over what their editors considered Willis' lack of good taste. Not only was Willis attacked in America; he also became involved in the preliminaries of a duel with Captain Frederick Marryat over the printing of a private letter which Willis had sent to Morris who inadvertently published it. The Tory critic John Gibson Lockhart made Willis the object of very strong attacks about his lack of good taste. Finally, in 1839 a difference between Morris and Willis, resulting from these criticisms, led to a break in the partnership.

The letter which caused Catholic readers to voice their displeasure was written from Rome and published in the *Mirror* on August 17, 1833, in which Willis made remarks about the wealth of Catholic cardinals. Referring to St. Peter's, he said that one would be reconciled to see the dome melted for alms and "his holiness reduced to a plain chapel and a rusty cassock."[54] Another letter printed on September 17, 1833, criticized the rites in Rome on Palm Sunday as "empty" and "absurd,"[55] described the Sistine Chapel as a scene of confusion, and criticized the private lives of clergymen in their association with women of society. Willis, of course, intended' the sketches to be gossipy, not anti-Catholic propaganda. The tenor of these essays would have found favor with militant Protestant groups in New York, for at the time there was strong animosity between Catholics and Protestants in the United States.[56] Morris disclaimed hostility toward the Catholic Church and came to Willis' defense.[57]

Two years later, Morris was placed in an embarrassing position by his author's statements in correspondence sent from London to the *Mirror.* When fellow editor Lewis Gaylord Clark, a friend of both Morris and Willis, referred to the incident in a letter to Henry Wadsworth Longfellow, Clark felt that Morris had not come to Willis' defense and had disclaimed responsibility for articles that had been written about certain figures in British society.[58]

In the *Mirror* issues of April 18 and 25, 1835, Willis, in a gossipy article about Lady Blessington, had given all the details of a soirée. Specifically, he had identified Tom Moore as a lover of Lady Blessington in her youth. In his fashion, Willis described Moore as a "Bacchus," as a worldling "who delighted in talking about the legs of a particular songstress."[59] As a consequence of the publication of Willis' article, strong opposition came from a few rival American editors. Clark pointed out to Longfellow: "Some of the newspapers, *National Intelligencer, Evening Post, Courier and Enquirer* are using up Willis tremendously, the latter especially." He continued: "They treat of his breaching of confidence, his want of honor, his un-American bias. Morris shrinks from his defense and says he is not responsible for what Willis says or does."[60]

The editor of the *Courier and Enquirer* accused Willis of pandering "to the low taste and the worse feelings of mankind." The editor of the *National Intelligencer* felt that he was endangering Anglo-American relations, and the *Post* editor said that his articles were written in "open violation of the laws of good breeding."[61]

V *Knickerbocker Editor*

It was evident that, after Morris' refusal to speak out, the seeds for future disagreement might exist. If sown, they lay dormant for a while. Willis continued working for the *Mirror*, and the differences between the partners were evidently forgotten. Only after four years of co-editorship was a *coup de grace* given in 1839 to the partnership as a result of another controversy that centered about the author. During the years abroad, Willis had become fairly well known as a correspondent and continued to keep in fairly close touch with literary coteries in England, writing about the latest social gossip and events which many American readers avidly awaited.

On October 20, 1838, Willis began a "New Series of Letters from London." One article of the series was signed "Veritas," and it included mention of a particular literary group. The passage in this article to which many American readers objected was about Letitia E. Landon, a writer whose work had been printed in the *Mirror* through the years and to whom Willis had referred in the *American Monthly*. The column discussed her relationships with William Jordan, English editor of the *Literary Gazette,* who had evidently influenced her poetry. The article, written in a sarcastic tone, suggested illicit relations with Jordan.[62]

Not long after this column appeared Morris felt called upon to make a public statement about the matter. Editorially, he apologized for the paragraph that was deemed objectionable by readers.[63] Lewis Gaylord Clark, in another letter to Longfellow, described the situation: "But 'the General' is getting his evil. Willis denounces him openly as a humbug in literature, and as a man, something worse than mean, which he cites as an especial characteristic."[64] This letter was written on January 7, 1839; by the end of the month Willis had severed connections with the *Mirror.* Almost immediately, he must have sent out notices announcing that he was to edit with T. O. Porter a new journal, the *Corsair.*[65]

This incident sparked another editorial barrage against Morris. In 1838, Park Benjamin, who had been connected with the *New England Magazine,* joined Horace Greeley's *New Yorker* as its literary editor. At the time of Willis' departure from the *Mirror,* the *New Yorker* felt that it was a great loss to the weekly. In May, 1839, the nature of the editorial remarks in the *Corsair* and the *New Yorker* might lead one to suspect that Benjamin and Willis had planned a campaign to bait Morris. It is more probable, however, that each man delighted in placing Morris on the defensive, for the latter prided himself on his propriety and his righteousness. The *New Yorker* criticized the *Mirror* for publishing objectionable material. An editorial referred to an Englishman writing for the *Mirror* who had "distinguished himself by lampoonery and slandering Miss Landon, the Countess of Blessington, and others." It further recommended that the *Mirror* be sent to Coventry "by everyone who held the name of woman in respect." It went on jokingly to lay total responsibility upon Morris and his journal "in which there never appeared a syllable to excite a blush upon the cheek of beauty."[66] It implied, in closing, that Morris was also the author of *Life in New York,* a religious tract which had purported to provide readers with moral tales about the evils of city life.

In a review of June 1, 1839, the *Corsair* joined forces with Benjamin, suggesting also that Morris was the author of the tract. The reviewer, tongue in cheek, even suggested that Morris himself had written the "gentlemanly reflections upon L.E.L. and others." Willis must have enjoyed the thought of Morris' discomfort. Taking the entire matter seriously, Morris vehemently denied the authorship; but the *Corsair* got in the last word by reasserting the charges.[67] Despite the differences between Willis and Morris, a reconciliation took place before the *Mirror* ended publication in 1842; for, in July of that year, the journal identified Willis as the "head of the new and popular school of lively and graphic sketches of fashionable and romantic life."[68]

In the summer of 1839, Willis sailed to Europe once again; this time his purpose was "to secure matter for his new magazine."[69] During this journey he met Thackeray, whose *Yellowplush* he had admired. On July 26, 1839, Willis wrote home to his co-editor that he had secured Thackeray's agreement for a "guinea a close column" to write letters for the periodical.[70] Thackeray did compose eight letters for the *Corsair* between July and October, but evidently ceased when payment was not forthcoming. Although this matter of non-payment cannot be firmly established, it is positive that Thackeray made a different kind of payment to Willis. On five occasions Thackeray aimed written barbs at the American author. As Professor Gordon Ray has pointed out, Thackeray satirized Willis in *Fraser's Magazine* in September, 1841, in "Notes on the North What-D-Ye-Callem Election, Being the personal narrative of Napoleon Putnam Wiggins, of Passimaquoddy."[71] Thackeray got more revenge when he wrote unfavorable reviews of Willis' books in 1845 and in 1850.[72]

Professor Harold H. Scudder has pointed out that the British author continued his satire even in *Vanity Fair*. In Chapter XLIX, Thackeray in writing about the personages whom Becky meets in the grand world, included a Mr. John Paul Jefferson Jones. The details of this character's life and personality match exactly with the facts of Willis' life.[73] And Thackeray did not cease then. There is no doubt that he had Willis, Morris, and the *Home Journal* in mind when in 1860 he wrote a passage for *The Adventures of Philip*. Philip, an English correspondent for the *Upper Ten Thousand Gazette* (the phrase "Upper Ten Thousand" was Willis' own), receives a recommendation to modify his letters: "By the way, your Philalethes' letters are not *quite spicy* enough, my worthy friend the Colonel says. They are *elegant and gay*, but the public here desires to have *more personal news; a little scandal about Queen Elizabeth,* you understand?"[74]

In 1840 the *Corsair* collapsed for want of financial support. Willis explained that the end of the publication was caused by the "multiplicity and importunity" of periodicals and by the backwardness "of a portion of the subscribing public...."[75] Actually, he had been long aware of the general situation which resulted in the folding of many weeklies and monthlies. He had offered his own reasons for the inadequate patronage of American journals while still editor of the *American Monthly*. Morris also repeatedly stressed the same explanation that the class of men who were in the pay of periodicals in England simply did not exist in the United States, nor was American patronage as great. Later in the 1830's colleagues of both Morris and Willis— such as Park Benjamin, James Fenimore Cooper, and Horace Greeley—commented upon the need for patronage. When the *Corsair* ended, Greeley commented upon Willis' ill fortune.

Early in the history of their magazine, Willis and Porter suggested to their readers why they had chosen that particular title. It had been their declared intention to "present as amusing a periodical as can be made from current wit, humor, and literature of the time." They had not hesitated in stating that they were going to employ English, French, and German belles-lettres and to use the "labors of Bulwer, Boz, Scribe, and Balzac because of the piratical law of copyright."[76] For Willis, the question of magazine patronage, remuneration of authors, plagiarism, pirating, and the need for an international treaty on copyright were clearly interrelated. Other journals such as the *Knickerbocker Magazine* and the *North American Review* had joined the *Evening Post* protesting against pirating in the 1820's.

During the 1830's, although Morris also had Theodore Fay and William Cox contributing essays and sketches to the *Mirror,* Willis exceeded all in popularity. All three authors were extremely able in composing "sketches" which seemed to be the right length for a journal that aimed to publish what was neither "too heavy nor too trivial." In addition to the letters and sketches, Willis' poems were also printed.

Possibly as a result of Willis' publishing much of his material abroad, Morris drew up articles of agreement with him which were signed on July 1, 1836. Specifically, Willis was to choose topics to write about which had proven popular in the *Mirror,* or to continue writing sketches of the scenes of his travel. Willis was to furnish weekly at least "ten of his usual Ms. pages ... and as much more as he can find leisure and material."[77] Willis served under the provisions of this contract until the two men dissolved the partnership.

What success the *Mirror* enjoyed in the 1830's was mainly due to the two editors. The *Mirror* had begun publication in the years of Irving's greatest popularity and continued under its dual editorship as part of the New York literary tradition. It published the works of New York writers, providing them with an outlet for their literary productions and giving them a wider audience than many of them had previously enjoyed. It published fictional and non-fictional literature about the Knickerbocker area in the manner of Irving—its history, its legends, its inhabitants, and its customs. The *Mirror* reported outstanding events of the city, as well as literary and cultural happenings. Lastly, it encouraged with well-chosen words the writers, the editors, the artists, the actors, and the musicians of the metropolis, offering them advice as the occasions suggested.

As a transmitter of the cultural efforts of the city and its environs, the *Mirror* also accomplished other important aims. It brought outstanding examples of the work of American and European writers to a New York audience. It served as an instrument of amusement and edification for many of the city's inhabitants.

Inextricably related to these accomplishments was the way in which the *Mirror* contributed to the development of a group of professional writers for journals ("magazinists" was the word Poe used). Willis' work was, of course, the best illustration of this development. His facile and deft style aided Morris in making the *Mirror* a "gossipy periodical." Many readers enjoyed the doings of the *haut monde* in London and New York. The opportunity offered by the weekly to read about the private lives and affairs of foreign littérateurs was no small factor in aiding circulation. Such reporting contributed ultimately to the establishment of a "cult of the fashionable" and to an "emulation of the elegant" by New York readers.

The editors' thorough knowledge of the city was another factor contributing to the success of the periodical. They were personally acquainted with all classes of New York's inhabitants—journalists, printers, doctors, actors, military men, politicians, authors, artisans, and artists. Departments of the journal invariably reflected readers' tastes. Dealing as it did with the "commonplace occurrences of society," matters of local interest, the weekly developed the tone of a town paper.

The two editors also were responsible in large measure for developing the weekly into a family journal. Within the tradition of the older magazines, they kept the *Mirror* a "repository of amusement and instruction" by designing sections to instruct the various members of the family in *utile dulci*. They brought the *Mirror* well along the path toward becoming a "home journal." Their devotion to the interests of women readers made it coincidentally an "elegant parlour journal" for the ladies. A student of American literature may see in the weekly a barometer of the contemporary reputation of certain writers, just as the historian may examine the issues for innumerable items on manners, prejudices, social customs, and tastes.

The life of the *Mirror* demonstrated that the reading public could support a literary journal, a principle in which Willis and Morris apparently never lost faith. The journal, at the same time that it followed certain elements of public taste, did in turn print material which over the years contributed to modifications of that taste. Leading public interest to matters literary was often not possible in the years before the *Mirror* flourished.

CHAPTER 3

Knickerbocker Journalist and
Bon Vivant

I New Editorships in New York

IN THE DECADES following the Jacksonian administration, the country underwent many social, economic, and political changes. For a separate but comparable series of causes, the journals with which Willis became associated also changed. The *Home Journal* that emerged in 1846 was a far different weekly in many respects from the *New York Mirror*. During the interval of years, Willis and Morris first published the *New Mirror* and then the *Weekly* and *Evening Mirrors*.

The two transformations, journalistic and national, were not completely unrelated. The modifications which Willis made in collaboration with Morris revealed certain changes in American journalism. The development of newspapers to be read by an ever widening popular, or mass, audience comprised part of this change. The accessibility of news to all citizens through the penny press characterized a journalistic revolution.[1] Editors had, therefore, a choice: they could aim to satisfy a national audience and attempt to answer the interests and tastes of a large reading public, or they could direct a specialized journal to a particular segment of the reading public. Willis, as co-editor of various journals, had to make a decision whether to print a daily or a weekly for a limited group of readers with special interests or one with wider popular features. Together, he and Morris discovered a satisfactory formula for publication from which they did not basically depart in their journals.

By April, 1843, the two former partners had completely forgotten past differences and difficulties. Actually, there was no recurrence of their separation; in fact, their friendship was broken only by Morris' death in 1864. In April, 1843, only three months had passed since the demise of the first *Mirror*. During this time the two journalists planned a new periodical, the *New Mirror*.

Morris' business sense made him cautious about publication costs for the new venture. For one thing, the *New Mirror* was reduced to octavo size. In the early months of publication, there was little dependence upon the work of any other writing journalist except Willis. The editors confessed that readers should know "that the two editors of this mirror of periodicals are not merely themselves, but several persons of notable industry."[2] They did, of course, reprint much material from the old *New York Mirror*.

The two men decided that, to increase its appeal to readers, "extras" or supplements to the *New Mirror* weekly editions would be published. This plan answered the competition of other weeklies, such as the *New World,* which had adopted the idea as a sales booster. As part of the plan to interest readers, they collaborated also on a series of imaginary and imaginative dialogues between Willis and the "Brigadier" (as he called Morris). These articles were artfully composed by Willis who adopted with great success the informal editorial approach which had earlier offended many of his Bostonian detractors in the *American Monthly Magazine*. The approach was also the same he had used when he had imitated the style of Christopher North. The *New Mirror* dialogues had their basis in fact and afforded readers glimpses behind the "paper curtains" of the editorial department. The series also served as a catch-all for many subjects. In the April 20, 1844, issue, the "cloister" (the editors' name for the editorial office) was pictured as crowded with "printers, engravers, stitchers, folders, advertisers, carriers, agents, and stereotypers."[3] Moreover, information about the editors' personal lives was sometimes included. Willis in light vein described the time when Morris had to go for a week's militia duty. Each Saturday was revealed as a day of intense activity in the *Mirror* office, when quick lunches were consumed by the editors in nearby Windust's Restaurant.[4] The editors showed also how publication problems were supposedly worked out. It was evident from the sketches that Willis was ever alert and fresh with ideas and sought the guidance, or the consolation, of Morris whom he used as a sounding board by reading him copy. Often, Willis revised articles by following his partner's suggestions.

Because the Post Office Department reclassified the *New Mirror* as a magazine, mailing rates were raised considerably. The editors naturally felt that the same postal rates should apply to both stitched and unstitched periodicals. Although the subscription list had risen to approximately eleven thousand by September, 1844, the editors regretfully announced the end of the *New Mirror* because of prohibitive costs of mailing. To avoid heavy postal rates, Willis and Morris planned to continue a journal in newspaper format.[5] The daily *Evening Mirror* made its debut on October 7, 1844. The *Weekly Mirror* appeared only a few days later on October 12. The daily was composed of four folio sheets with seven solid columns of print on each page, and advertising was placed on the third and fourth pages.

At this time, Willis and Morris asked a third man, Hiram Fuller, to become their partner. Economic reasons dictated this decision. According to a signed agreement, Morris and Willis were to continue editing the journal and directing its literary department, respectively. The announced separation of functions was, in fact, not strictly followed. When Willis went to Europe in 1845, Morris administered the literary sections.

No place in the journal did either Willis or Morris refer to the men with whom they worked. Evidence exists, however, which shows that there is the strongest possibility that in 1844 both Walt Whitman and Edgar Allan Poe may have been working on the *Mirror*'s staff. Professor Gay Wilson Allen, Whitman's biographer, mentions his working for the *Mirror* for two or three weeks in October, 1844.[6] Poe apparently joined the staff the same month.[7]

While Willis was in Europe early in 1845, Morris finally dissociated himself from the journal because of Fuller's involvement in the war of the New York literati. Poe, a strong antagonist of Fuller, explained to a fellow editor that Willis and Morris had learned of a swindling action in which Fuller had been involved.[8] Not long after this time Morris decided to begin a new publication called the *National Press.*

II *The Association with Poe*

Any examination of the life of Edgar Allan Poe reveals that his detractors during his lifetime outnumbered those who praised him. Of all his literary or journalist associates, there was hardly one with whom he did not quarrel. Two noteworthy exceptions were Nathaniel P. Willis and George Pope Morris, for both men were consistent in their kind treatment of Poe. On all occasions, Poe reciprocated their friendship.

The two editors recognized Poe's abilities and accorded his work favorable comment throughout his writing career, with the exception of Willis' rejection of an early poem for the *American Monthly.* Although the facts of Poe's life are generally well-known, one should briefly examine the nature of his relationship with these men. In 1831, the *New York Mirror* had praised the edition of Poe's poetry that was published.[9] The *Mirror* saw merit in his short stories and lauded his *Tales of the Grotesque and Arabesque.*[10] On his part, Poe praised the *Mirror* and its editors in an article that he contributed to *Alexander's Weekly Magazine,*[11] and—as has been suggested—he "perhaps at this time would not have been adverse to being connected with the *Mirror.*"[12]

Morris and Willis did much more than simply recognize Poe's genius: they gave him employment when he was in need of funds.[13] Moreover, they provided on occasion a market for his poems and a medium for his criticism. After he joined the staff of the *Evening Mirror,* he continued working for it as a sub-editor and as "mechanical paragraphist" until January, 1845, when he left only because he had the opportunity to become editor of the *Broadway Journal.* Willis recalled in a letter, which he wrote to Morris on October 27, 1858, that Poe had helped them both during the "harassing and exhausting days of 'daily' editorship." Poe, Willis felt, must have been aware that his job with the *Mirror* was a "step downward" after his experience as a "chief editor of several monthlies."[14] In his job for Willis and Morris, Poe wrote and secured material for the miscellaneous columns of the *Evening Mirror.* After Poe's death, Willis praised his conduct during this period as exemplary. Willis regarded him as a most gentlemanly person who proved himself "invariably punctual and industrious."[15]

Poe translated from the French for the two editors, although one of his biographers wrongly attributed all the stories initialed "E.P." to Poe. Actually, most of them were done by an Emily Percival although Poe did identify for Mrs. Sarah Helen Whitman one or two of them as his work.[16] No articles appeared over his signature during the period, and it may be assumed that he was busy daily with routine hack work and probably had very little time for creative composition. Temporarily, at least, he was given some relief from his financial situation.

While working in the *Mirror* office, Poe was "solemnly summoned" by Willis to examine critically the subject of adequate pay for American authors, a topic in which Willis was interested since the beginning of his editorial career in the late 1820's. Poe's essays appeared in the *Evening Mirror* in October, 1844, and in January, 1845.[17] In January, two other important Poe items appeared. First, he began a series of critical articles in which he accused Longfellow of plagiarism, a literary event which was later often referred to as the "Longfellow War."[18] Second, "The Raven" made its first appearance the same month in the *Mirror*.[19]

When Poe left the staff to work full time with the *Broadway Journal*, Morris had already left the editor's chair to the partner remaining, Hiram Fuller. Morris explained his departure to Fuller by stating that he intended to go into business. During January, Poe knew that he was to leave the *Mirror;* and, since he held a job which involved the composition of miscellaneous items and the arrangement of columns in the daily, he took advantage of the opportunity to publicize his own work. A brief article appeared on January 14 referring to his "The Literary Life of Thing-um Bob Esq." Throughout the month other items appeared.[20]

Toward the end of January, 1845, a benefit was held in New York for George Pope Morris. Poe attended and reported the event in detail. At a later date, Willis explained that he had knowledge of Morris' being in danger of losing the ownership of his home because of a series of financial reverses. Willis had actually made plans for such a benefit late in 1844; but Morris declined to be so honored when he heard of the benefit. The January affair, however, was held and netted about two thousand dollars, a sum which allowed Morris to pay his creditors and keep his home. Willis' concern for Morris' financial straits recalls his earlier attempt to solicit funds for Poe, whose illness he had publicized on the pages of the *Home Journal*. Although Poe was embarrassed by the announcement, both he and Mrs. Clemm praised Willis' generosity.

During the remaining years of Poe's life, Willis and Morris continued to comment favorably upon his work in the *Home Journal*. Shortly after Poe's death in October, 1849, Willis wrote a highly laudatory article to counteract what the Reverend Rufus Griswold had said about the author in the *Tribune* obituary.[21] Through Willis' comments, one gets a glimpse of Poe at his best—a writer and a magazinist capable of sustained application to his work and a person grateful for the kindnesses shown him. Later, George Graham, for whom Poe had worked, wrote to Willis underlining the truth of Willis' appraisal and condemning the lies of Griswold.

In the *Literati* papers, Poe made separate evaluations of the two editors who had befriended him. Extremely fair in his criticism, he did not allow his personal feelings to interfere with the exercise of his critical judgment. Poe's balanced evaluation did not exceed in the direction either of rancor or of "puffing."

III *Magazine of the "Upper Ten"*

In 1844, after the *New Mirror* had attained a circulation of ten thousand, Willis labeled the magazine as the periodical of the "upper ten thousand," a phrase which caught on among readers and the literati.[22] The prospectus re-emphasized his intention of writing tales which would show the distinctions of society. The decision to emphasize society reporting was a significant one. Subscribers' requests undoubtedly influenced the editors in deciding about the course they were to take as society journalists.

Willis justified his attention to society by an editorial statement: "The barriers which exist abroad between those whom nature would not have separated, are fast forming in our country, and all light thrown upon the tendencies of our national character while in progress of formation will be more useful than amusing."[23] Since the public's interest in the earlier group of essays which contained much gossip about the British literati had proven a stimulus to sales, Morris and Willis logically hoped that a stress upon similar subject matter in the new publication would have as great an appeal. Morris as business editor sensed this strongly. During the years of the *New York Mirror,* both men had wanted to give their journal an air of hauteur as a fashionable parlor magazine. All these factors now combined in the editors' decision to become the spokesmen of the cult of the fashionable.

In June, 1843, as part of a discussion of fashion, Willis wrote a significant comment about social classes in America: "Part the extremes—widen the distance between wealth and poverty—and you make room for a *middle class* . . . everybody who is not absolutely poor, striving to seem absolutely rich. Of this middle class, literary men are a natural part and parcel. So are many of the worthiest and most intelligent people of this country."[24] It was, in reality, to this group that Willis and Morris addressed themselves in their magazines in the 1840's and 1850's.

The editors continued their policy of paying special attention to the fashionable and social world. They came to regard themselves as purveyors of cultivation and refinement. They advised the public on one occasion that they "had the means of knowing what taste and elegance are doing in the world."[25]

As they had with the *New York Mirror,* they placed themselves consciously in the tradition of the *Tatler* and of Irving's work by determining to report any foibles of society: "If there is a paper which would appeal to both high and low republican—amusing itself without fear or favor with the follies of the conspicuously foolish, and hammering without flinching at the brutalities of the vicious vulgar . . . it is the Evening Mirror."[26]

One editorial revealed that they felt it necessary to assure readers that they did not consider themselves as members of a group apart. They had been successful with the *New York Mirror* by instructing readers without appearing to patronize them. The editors offered this explanation of their policy:

We are not recording this view of things i.e. reporting events in society by way of assuming to be, ourself, above this everyday level of the public mind—too superfine to be a part of such a public. Not a bit of it. We cannot afford superfinery of any kind. We are trying to make a living by being foremost in riding on a coming turn of the tide. . . . the taste for refinements, for distinctions, for aristocratic entrenchments—is nearing with the additional momentum of a recoil.[57]

Reporting taste and refinement became their distinctive stock in trade; as the self-appointed instructors, they had to reassure the public, the instructed, that they as editors were not members of any social élite. Verbally, the statement might be interpreted as something of a retreat; but in practice Willis and Morris did not modify the policy of the papers, or change the contents of their articles. With the avowed purpose of reporting "town society," they printed translated articles on French fashion and society and published reports of the doings of the English *haut monde*. Representative columns were labeled: "Gossip of French Newspapers," "Parisian Chit-Chat," "Paris Fashions," and "Outlines of Topics in Late French Papers."[28] Much of this material had already been printed in French in the *Courrier des États-Unis*, published in New York. It was probably such material that Poe translated for Willis.

Before the time of Willis' departure for Europe in June, 1845, the *Evening Mirror* established a column "Town and Country" which was to include the reports of doings at the favorite American society resorts.[29] The title unknowingly anticipated the name of the magazine which would ultimately (in the twentieth century) succeed the *Home Journal*, the editors' next and last journalistic effort.

IV *Mirrors of Popular Taste*

Although the two men paid increasing attention to reporting the fashionable world, their editorial policy varied in regard to political material. In the *Evening Mirror*, they had declared neutrality of treatment. In the same paper they had asserted that they would "point at the abuses by either party of the freedom of press and speech, means or influence."[30] Within New York City itself, they strove to be fair to the journals of both political parties. For example, in May, 1843, the editors were particularly struck by an issue of the *Democratic Review* and observed that it possessed the "rare merit of uniting a powerful advocacy of party interests and principles with a high literary tone." They were careful to mention in the same issue that the *Knickerbocker* (edited by Whig Lewis Gaylord Clark) had an Editor's Table that always gave readers a "feast of good things."[31] Their striving after neutrality in politics even carried over into their column, "Advice to Contributors." In July, 1845, when contributions were solicited, they recommended that authors write "seasonable articles" with the caveat, however, that they eschew "feverish subjects" such as the annexation of Texas and of Oregon. They felt that the very mention of these questions was likely to "produce war fever in excitable temperaments."[32]

The editors promised that their papers would be "responsible indices of public opinion." They promised, moreover, that they would "let no political topic go without the best handling" they could give to it.[33] Political news in the papers consisted of the publication verbatim of official dispatches, political speeches of both parties, and essays on political subjects. Despite the fact that the *Mirror* printed essays both for and against annexation, the editors were fearful of a war of conquest and revealed opinions similar to those who opposed annexation, the "locofoco" Democrats. The editors justified a declaration of their opinions by asserting that they were not expressing party views. The problem of annexation, they felt, was "too high a question to be discussed on mere party grounds."[34] Contrary to their own advice, they did not "eschew this feverish subject" but stated, regarding the matter, "It [the problem] is one which affects the *honor* of the *whole country,* for (mystify as we may) our government will be regarded as *first sanctioning the invasion of a weak neighbor by its armed citizens, and their sharing in the plunder.*"[35] Later, they modified their stand and praised President Polk after he had declared a hope for annexation only through negotiation.[36] They felt that he was pursuing a "lofty policy."

Willis and Morris felt that, as a result of their declared neutrality, they were better qualified than members of the partisan press in "pronouncing upon the practice of removing people from political office."[37] In a straightforward editorial, "The Outrages against the Mormons," the *Mirror* condemned the Ohio mob whose action had resulted in the death of Mormon leader Joseph Smith.[38]

Both editors never forgot, however, that their periodical was mainly "literary." In the *Evening Mirror,* they pointed out to their readers that literature was no "longer shelved or dusty." To the editors it had become an "everyday matter."[39] One editorial statement is significant: *"To make literature even footed with business and pleasure* is a demand of the times, and by *making literature a feature of a daily newspaper,* this demand seems promptly and effectually answered."[40]

In addition to printing dramatic and musical reviews in their daily and weekly, the editors printed literary notices of new publications. Despite the fact that "one of the worst sins of our newspaper press" was the manner in which new works were noticed, the editors in this respect did little to set an example for others to follow. Although they vowed that the critical department would be discriminating in judgments and statements, there is no evidence that practice followed policy.[41] Most notices had no more than a few words of information about the books published.

During this period, they probably became two of the most active attendants at various literary soirées, many held in the home of Miss Anne Lynch on Waverly Place. Both editors had known Miss Lynch in the 1830's, but not until the early 1840's did she become a central figure of the New York literary coteries. At her home, they met Herman Melville, although it was Morris who attended the stag dinners at Evert Duyckinck's. Despite the fact that neither Morris nor Willis identified themselves with the "Young America" group of whom Duyckinck was a spokesman, there was one issue on which they agreed—the international copyright treaty.

In August, 1845, Willis and Morris found it necessary to secure a copyright for newly written material composed for the *Mirror* as a protection against domestic pirating. The editors had always been strong advocates of an international copyright treaty and had never hesitated to recommend it. They, in fact, criticized statesmen for not espousing the cause,[42] and it was they who had asked Poe to write on the problem. What Poe wrote significantly applied to Willis' situation upon which he himself had expressed opinions many times before. Poe pointed out that editors had depended heavily upon the editor's pen and voluntary contributions. An unpromising literary market had thereby been created for authors who would normally be in a position to sell their material. Such authors unfortunately found editors accepting the contributions of "females" and "other facile writers" who gave away their material.[43] Poe cited the earlier *New York Mirror* as an example of a magazine that had followed this practice. Discretion probably dictated his not mentioning the periodical for which he was working as another example.[44] It was indeed ironic that Willis and Morris, who deplored inadequate pay for authors, had been continually obliged for economic reasons to depend heavily upon contributed articles and the production of editors' pens; in some measure they thereby worsened a condition they condemned.

The editors indeed never lacked contributions. Just two months after the first issue of the *New Mirror,* the editors begged for mercy; they had received nearly three hundred separate poems. Since they could neither print this many nor pay for them, they advised the "poets" to work over and improve their contributions.[45] Poems printed in the *Mirror* were often by such authors as Longfellow or Poe, whose reputations were well established.

In 1843, the editors had realized that "the republic of letters" was "fast coming under female dominion."[46] *Godey's Lady's Book* was singled out as a "powerful gynocracy." As both Willis and Morris catered to feminine tastes in the *New York Mirror,* they accepted in the later periodicals the work of many more women contributors who had established reputations as writers. Anna Cora Mowatt, Frances S. Osgood, and Anne Lynch were three members of the New York literary group whose work most frequently appeared in the *Evening* and *Weekly Mirrors.* In addition, there were poems by Lydia Maria Child and by Maria Brooks.[47] Willis had earlier recognized the ability of a young apprentice in the *New Mirror's* printing office, Bayard Taylor—whom Augustus Duganne, a contemporary satirist, lampooned as the protégé of "Natty" Willis.[48]

Probably the most prominent writer for the *Evening* and *Weekly Mirrors* other than Willis was "Fanny Forester." In June, 1844, a Miss Emily Chubbock—a teacher of Utica, New York, and a random contributor of verses to periodicals—wrote a short sketch and sent it to the *New Mirror* editors. They recognized her ability and solicited more contributions. For many weeks her short, sentimental, chatty sketches appealed to readers. Very early, Willis commended her work to the publishers of *Graham's* and of *Godey's.* As a direct result, she became one of the most popular contemporary writers of sketches for these magazines.

V   *Sophisticated, Sentimental, and Saleable*

With the *New Mirror* publications in 1843 and 1844, Willis and
Morris proved that they could successfully regain an audience
after undergoing financial mishaps with the *Corsair* and the *New
York Mirror.* Through careful economizing, they sustained publication. They also allowed themselves greater flexibility in editorial policy. The minor changes in composition which they readily made reflected what they considered shifts in the tastes of the
reading public. Inadequate funds unfortunately made them rely
heavily in many issues upon the use of scissors and paste. Their
fellow editor Park Benjamin truthfully observed that some issues
lacked originality since columns were often filled with reprints
of old material.

Before circumstances forced an end to the *New Mirror,* Willis
had nearly succeeded in making the periodical a "society journal." Despite the desire to enlarge circulation by appealing to
many groups of a reading public, the editors felt that they could
most successfully direct their efforts toward producing a journal
of interest to those who would pay to read about the world of
fashion and society. Two decades earlier, they would not have
been able to thus specialize. The large increase in the size of
the population of New York City and the increase in the numbers of a moderately well-off middle class provided the names
for the subscription list. During the years of the last *Mirrors,* they
strove to hold a family audience as subscribers by making the
periodicals journals for the home. They catered to devotees of
the "elegant," but always in words which reflected adherence to
a strict standard of gentility. Men less able to attune themselves
to the public taste would have had difficulty in detecting the
exact line between gossip reporting and scandalmongering.

The simple question of journalistic survival had earlier required Morris and Willis to revise the *New Mirror.* Before the
Post Office Department forced the issue, they had given consid-
eration to the idea of printing a newspaper. When they finally
decided to convert their journal to a daily and a weekly, they
carried over to the new periodicals essentially the same principles
and policies of publication. In changing the format, the editors
felt that they would be able to match the penny press in the
appeal of their folio edition, and yet within these fewer pages to

retain the literary quality of their earlier publications. This practice of issuing both a daily and a weekly provided them with valuable experience. They learned that reporting of politics almost inevitably led to unexpected developments and disputes, and to compromises of the neutrality upon which they had prided themselves.

Before Hiram Fuller subverted the papers to his own policies, the editors had finally come to a formula of successful publication. Their paper was to be an instrument for cultivation and refinement appealing to American readers who aspired to self-improvement in manners. Their journal was to be an arbiter of fashion, a reflector and yet a creator of taste. They sought to keep alive in their readers too a feeling for a "literature of the town." Readers were able to enjoy vicariously all the events on the city's social and literary calendars. The editors were generally successful in making their publications both sophisticated and sentimental, saleable to a large middle-class reading public.

The comment of Park Benjamin made a few days after the first appearance of the *Evening Mirror* was equally applicable during its existence while Willis and Morris were connected with it: "It is as tasteful and sightly an affair as was to have been expected from the well-known 'savoir-faire' of our friends Messrs Morris and Willis."[49]

CHAPTER 4

Teller of Tales

I *Magazinist*

W ILLIS' talent for writing the sketch and the short story matched his ability as a narrator of travel essays. Many of his stories derive from experiences described in the essays which he sent back to the *New York Mirror* from the Near East, the Continent, and England. Other tales are based upon his travels in New York State and Canada. Thoroughly interested in places and people, he had kept a detailed diary of his impressions of his 1827 trip. Shortly after the journey to Canada, he began composing sketches about his travels. It was also his habit, one begun during his collegiate days, to assemble quotations and passages for his scrapbooks. He read avidly and recorded items of interest, copying excerpts from the works which appealed to him. Three sources of experience—travel, reading, and reflection—provided material for his writing.

As editor of the *Legendary*, the *Token*, and the *American Monthly Magazine*, he conveniently published his own work until 1831. Later, as co-editor of the *New York Mirror*, he altered many of his earlier works and reprinted the modified sketches and stories. While writing a large number of short narratives, he aspired to write a longer work of fiction; but it was not until 1856 that he managed to complete a full-length novel, *Paul Fane*.

In writing his fictionalized sketches, Willis followed the tradition of Washington Irving and in the wake of the popularity of the *Sketch Book*. Irving had succeeded because he, as Professor Quinn has pointed out, combined in his work the "narrative objective tale" and the "subjective essay of character."[1] Of the writers influenced by Irving in the pre-Civil War period, and they were numbered by the score in New York, Willis was unquestionably the most popular and the most successful. He employed Irving's approach in writing his sketches, and the titles of Willis' collections indicate the debt. In place of "Sketches" by Geoffrey Crayon there were "Inklings" by Phil Slingsby (the name of Willis' narrator is taken from Irving).[2] Indeed, when Willis' entire range of stories is surveyed, one finds that he equaled Irving's accomplishment many times in the composition of both non-fictional sketches and travelogues. He frequently matched Irving in the quality of his short stories. At other times, however, the structure of Willis' stories was weak, and often plot and characterization were incompletely developed.

Willis had already revealed his penchant for writing witty commentaries about social life and for treating in a light, humorous vein the situations in which he placed his characters. He had created such characters as Cousin Sybil, the most patient of listeners; his dandified friend Tom Lascelles; and an anonymous bibliophile with whom he carried on conversations about writing. As one examines Willis' fictional work, it may be useful to note the statements that he made about writing. These observations are scattered through reviews, editorials, and, later, in prefaces to various collections of his work. In the *American Monthly Magazine* of November, 1829, he expressed his basic opinion that "Literature . . . [was] mainly a heightened picture of human nature."[3] The object of writing was to represent the features of men so that they might know themselves better. From the beginning of his career, Willis particularly wanted to write about Society and to catch "the careless and fleeting changes of expression" of the members of the *haut monde.* He tried often, he said, to transmit the tenor of witty conversation among the *bon vivants.*

As a practical editor and writer, he offered advice to aspiring authors. He stressed the point that "periodical readers expect to be amused."[4] He therefore suggested that writers should cultivate humor. He recommended brevity as a cardinal principle for authors. He stated succinctly that a magazine article should never exceed six pages. Although Willis wrote this advice for those who would be magazinists, he also expressed repeatedly his regrets that many would-be novelists were forced away from composing in this genre because of the absence of both an American copyright law and an international copyright treaty.

He made other observations about his work. He readily admitted that for many of his stories and sketches he relied on his memory more than on his imagination. In this manner, he attempted to justify shortcomings in structure. In the Preface to *Inklings of Adventure* he wrote: "The dramas of real life are seldom well-wound up, and the imperfectness of plot which might be objected to them as tales, will prove to the observant reader that they are drawn more from memory than fancy."[5] A decade later in the prefatory remarks to *Dashes at Life*, Willis confessed that marketableness required him to break what he had planned as longer stories into short ones.[6] The briefer structure of the tales for periodicals, he repeated, was required by "copyright and necessity." He did positively hope, however, to "achieve truth to life."[7] He ultimately pleaded a devotion to realism as an excuse for making commentaries and digressions within the stories themselves.

In the Preface to *People I Have Met,* he anticipated George Eliot's introductory remarks in *Middlemarch.* "Real life," he wrote, "is not as commonplace as it is presented"; for there are "invisible little dramas in the world."[8] He believed that fiction had its compensations, for a writer could very often achieve a greater "fidelity to portraitures in a story." The author would also be "able to draw portions of the inner life" which were denied to him in writing a biography.[9]

Willis, in remarks incorporated in the collected *Prose Works,* made a general distinction between tales and "fun-jottings." The latter, however, merely constitute variants of tales as interpreted by his contemporaries. "Fun-Jottings" were about "turns of event or of character which have amused" him. Professor Pattee has made what is a clearer distinction in describing the two types of short fiction in which Willis excelled: "the light prose narrative shortened for the popular magazine was a sketch lighter than a tale."[10] Kendall B. Taft, the literary historian of the Knickerbocker writers, has cited a review which appeared in 1825 in which an author pointed out that a tale required ". . . great vivacity of narration, and more point and polish of style."[11]

In the Preface to *Rural Letters,* Willis identified what he had considered as the requirements placed upon an author who chose to write a short story: "No one who has tried this vocation can have any idea of the difficulty of procuring the light, yet condensed,—the fragmented, yet finished,—the good tempered and gentlemanly, yet high seasoned and dashing, papers necessary to a periodical. A man who can write them in our country, put himself to a more profitable use—and does."[12] Willis admitted that he "had tried life in every shape, . . . [he] had studied human nature under all the changes which can be wrought by differences of climate, rank, culture, and association."[13]

II *Sketcher in the Irving Tradition*

Willis began the publication of sketches and stories in the *Legendary.* "Leaves from a Colleger's Album," which appeared in the second volume, relied heavily upon his travel experiences during the year he graduated from Yale. This sketch is the forerunner of all his fiction in which he used, in part, a collegiate locale.[14] Willis created a circle of young men who are representative types: Horace Fritz, the dandy; Charles Wimbledon, a "prince of good fellows"; and Job Clark, a giant, awkward country lad. The slight plot revolves about an excursion to Niagara Falls; the story is told, in part, in the form of letters received from members of the group. Job's letter, for example, reveals the writer as a "pure, unsophisticated Vermont boy." Horace is shown as a practical joker, for he succeeds in having Job pass himself off as a Universalist minister to an unsuspecting group of countryfolk in upstate New York.

Later, Willis used sections of "Leaves" for a two-part story, "Letters of Horace Fritz," published in the *American Monthly Magazine.*[15] Here, Horace writes of Job Clark whose release from the position of schoolmaster permits him to take a trip with the narrator. In the story, Willis included details of his impressions of Geneva, New York, as well as reflections upon the beauty of natural scenery. The second "Letter" continues the travelogue relating Tom's and Job's stay in Ithaca and a delightful description of a Sunday camp meeting. Later in the chronicle, the two travelers return to the Erie Canal, continue their trip to Rochester, and catch glimpses en route of a few Indians and settlers in the isolated regions.

After the stories in the *Legendary*, Willis edited the *Token*, including his own productions. "The Ruse" was among these selections. Philip Blondel, the main character of this tale, is, without doubt, a reflection of Willis himself. The fictional character is described as handsome, but not effeminate; "popular in society"; "excellent in conversation." He also has a "refined disinterestedness in the trifles of everyday intercourse."[16] The light plot involves Alice Blair, with whom Philip has fallen in love, and a Mr. Skefton who is a priggish city-bred rival. Although Skefton plans to marry Alice, she (through a ruse) writes down Philip's name as the groom in a note to the minister. Philip is delighted to be expelled from college because of his marriage, and the story ends on a humorous note. As if prophesying his own reception at the hands of critics, he speaks of the popular man as one who is not sensitive, "for he must stand quizzery."[17]

The pages of the *American Monthly* give readers today a complete sampling of the tales and sketches which the author later composed in the 1830's and 1840's. These selections are also important because a few are variants of stories which he reworked and of themes to which he returned repeatedly. When Willis composed in 1836 an introduction to *Inklings of Adventure,* he stated that many of the incidents about which he spun a story were taken from a "rambling notebook of his own."[18] The sketches which appeared in the *American Monthly* were drawn from this notebook. The title of one of these productions about his Canadian and New York trip anticipated the title of the 1836 collection, "An Inkling of an Adventure." The notes supplied him with material for two installments of "Notes upon a Ramble" (which served as a basis for later stories) and of "Pencillings by the Way" (which was composed in diary fashion), including highly impressionistic descriptions of what he saw in Canada. Two other essays should be mentioned: "Minute Philosophies" and "Unwritten Music." Both are reflective in tone, written in an Addisonian vein. The remaining pieces appearing in the *American Monthly* may generally be divided into romances and humorous sketches of manners.

Willis told "An Inkling of an Adventure" in the first person, about an incident supposedly occurring at Lake George, New York, when a family asks the narrator to share its boat on an extended sight-seeing trip on the lake. He employed a fictionalized framework for including comments about the scenery: "I think I am 'in' for a description. I don't very well see how I can let you off without it. If I were to report the gay conversation around the tiller, it would not be at all the same thing as the sweet toned bagetelle...."[19] The narrator continued by admitting that a description of the lake would "eke out the story and save" him from the dilemma of trying to reproduce delightful conversation since he admitted that he did not want to set down a dialogue constructed from "clear fancy."[20] In the story, the kind hosts never reveal their names; and, unfortunately, the narrator never meets them again. He searches for them at various resorts, but he is identified at the conclusion as a sort of "traveling Tantalus" for he points out: "There is no denouement."[21]

The other sketches which constituted "Notes upon a Ramble" were published in the April and June, 1830, issues of the *American Monthly Magazine*. The first installment about Willis' journey on Lake Ontario and on the St. Lawrence River relates the incidents aboard a ship which is carrying a British regiment back to England. These recollections provided the author with the source for tales submitted to British magazines in the mid-1830's. The second of the series continues a narration of the journey and presents in graphic detail reactions to people and places in Montreal and Quebec.[22]

Two other sketches which combine elements of the essay and the tale are "A Winter Scene in New England" and "A Morning in the Library."[23] The first, with its extended reflection upon seasonal changes, recalls Irving since it contains passages of excellent description of nature. "A Morning in the Library," a narrative told in the first person, introduces, in the manner of his own "Tête-à-Tête Confessions" and "The Scrapbook," a careful listener in the person of Florence to whom the narrator lightly discourses upon the benefits of idleness.

One of the tales which followed the sentimental tradition closely is "The Death of the Gentle Usher."[24] Willis used Yale College as the setting for a story about a precocious, but ill, student Clement Revere. The narration suffers from a preciousness of tone since the main character's emotions are described in excessive detail. The depiction of Revere's death is ultra-sentimental.[25] Another tale—or more correctly collection of three tales —which is much more successfully written is "Incidents in the Life of a Quiet Man," supposedly drawn from collegiate experiences. He was later to modify the work, presenting the three incidents separately. The well-done earlier versions are narrated with a minimum of elaboration. An introduction identifies the narrator as one who acted as a nurse for fellow students who needed medical attention. The tales are in the Gothic tradition, respectively about a vigil with a corpse, "a mad senior," and the pursuit of a friend struck by moon-madness. Each story succeeds in establishing an atmosphere of eeriness or horror, not unlike Poe's tales in this respect. The following passage from the first story is representative:

> I could see down into the town, and far along the streets on either side of the common, and there was not a figure to darken the white sidewalks, and I listened until my ear was pained with silence, and could not hear even a dog's bark. I turned from the window with an undefined feeling of dread, and looking at my patient, replenished the fire, and sat down again to my book. I had read perhaps half a page, when he rose suddenly in the bed. . . . [26]

His other romances were not so successful; of the five which appeared in the *American Monthly Magazine*, it is a credit to his critical taste that he reprinted only one, which he retitled and reconstructed. "Confessions of a Disliked Man" is a maudlin story which attempts to recapture through first-person narration the details of loneliness of a self-centered misanthrope.[27] "The Exile," about the settlement of French emigrés in the New World, is only slightly more successful. The relationship to the sentimental romance is evident: "The incidents we are about to relate are rather of a simpler character than usual, and yet they may amuse those readers even in this age of startling romance, who retain some quiet corner of their hearts for sympathy and feeling."[28] The two emigrés, husband and wife, live in an Arcadian locale on the edge of a New York lake. They are discovered there by a friend of the girl's father. In the narration, Willis included enough French passages to suggest authenticity. The two emigrés relate the details of their flight from France; after hearing their story, the older friend offers them asylum and the hospitality of his home. The closing scene takes the reader ahead by many years: the emigrés have returned to France and have had their properties returned to them.

Another story dealing with European exiles, "Baron Von

Raffleoff," provided Willis with material for a later story, "Pedlar Karl."[29] In the earlier version, the romance anticipated many stories that the author was to write about life at American social resorts. Among its *dramatis personae* is Willis' friend of the *American Monthly* editorials, Tom Lascelles. The story contains many observations about social life at an American summer resort, but the plot centers about Lord C—— and Meeta, a beautiful young woman who is the object of attention of an unusual pedlar. The narrator becomes a very close friend of the young lady whose conversation, he finds, always returns to guesses about the pedlar's identity. The denouement reveals the pedlar as a romantic young German student who has followed his love to America. He succeeds in eloping with Meeta with the help, ironically, of the narrator who had earlier felt jealousy toward the pedlar.

"The Elopement" is more digression than story. Having introduced readers to members of the *beau monde* who are looking over gloves in a fashion shop, Willis comments at length upon miscellaneous social matters in Boston and New York, with an apostrophe to Gotham. Although it is placed within a light context, one passage contained Willis' own feelings: "Here [Boston] every body knows every body, and his business. You cannot stir without feeling your importance. A very little stranger makes a 'very splendid tiger,' and a peculiar tie in a cravat gives you three months' immortality. Your birth, religion, early history, finances, and probabilities transpire with your arrival."[30] What remains of the story is a proposal of elopement to Cecile, one of two sisters, by the foppish Hyperion St. John. All is arranged for the trip until Cecile receives a *billet-doux*, composed in atrocious spelling, that is sufficient cause to her for declining the "honor."

A story told in as light a vein is "The Fancy Ball."[31] Willis approached obvious parody of the light romantic tale so popular with women readers: "It goes to my heart to tell a story right on like a newspaper. The days of romance are gone, however, and the poetry that used to be trolled to the tinkle of guitar under my lady's window, is now written with a slate and pencil, and the teller of tales is positively expected to be intelligible and preserve some faint resemblance to nature."[32] The body of the story is taken up with the characterizations of Gerald Gray and of

Helen and Cecile, two sisters. The plot is mainly derived from his mixed emotions toward the sisters. Light patter about a fancy-dress ball completes another main portion of the story. Cecile's anger at Gerald's attitude, or his pique at her coolness—of such thin threads is the fabric of the story woven. As a climax, Gerald proposes to Helen and rationalizes his change of heart; for he had planned to marry Cecile. Willis leaves the story without denouement by not revealing the contents of Helen's final letter to Gerald, but the author solicits readers to inquire if they are anxious about the story's final resolution.

The lightness of tone and the sense of the comic evident in "The Elopement" and in "The Fancy Ball" become dominant features in other stories. "The Last Bachelor" tells of a group of friends resolving at New Year's Eve that the last of the group remaining unmarried will have to drink a bottle of vinegar by himself. In this story Willis succeeded by artful use of dialogue in characterizing the individuality of each member of the group. In the conclusion, Tom, the last bachelor, reads the letters of his married friends. The discontent of his friends makes his own bachelorhood appear sweeter despite "vinegar drinking."[33]

"Albina McLush" was one of the most successful humorous stories. A plump, lethargic woman, Albina is the opposite of everything "dainty" or "spirituelle." In the manner of travesty, the narrator describes her immobility and her "imperial indifference." Finally, seizing the unusual moment when Albina seems alert, he offers her his hand in marriage only to "find Miss McLush asleep." Actually, in this tale, he parodied one of his own poems, "The Annoyer."[34]

Three of the stories published at this period depend for their climaxes upon situations involving mistaken identity: "The Alias—or Mr. St. John," "Captain Thompson," and "Driving Stanhope Pro Tem." In the first Mr. R——, the narrator, sunburnt and unkempt, is introduced inopportunely to his friend's sister. Later, dressed and appearing completely different, he is not recognized by the young lady, and he proceeds to pass himself off as "a Mr. St. John." Finally, as Mr. R——, he addresses Gertrude, the friend's sister, who asks for his opinion of Mr. St. John. The story ends delightfully with Gertrude's finally being informed of the identity of both.[35] The second story introduces Phil Slingsby, who becomes interested in a young mother who is traveling on the same stage coach. He finds that she is headed for Boston to meet her seafaring husband, a Captain Thompson. Volunteering his services in helping her, he discovers a Captain Thompson at one hotel and is peremptorily thrown out by the irate seaman. Phil, however, does succeed in reuniting the family for there is, in fact, another Captain Thompson. Again, the action moves along swiftly; Willis succeeds in picturing for readers Mrs. Thompson's young child with sticky fingers climbing over the narrator's white waistcoat.[36] The third of the series, "Driving Stanhope, Pro Tem," tells of a misadventure in which Phil Slingsby appears. He borrows the carriage of a friend and is mistakenly suspected as a thief in a town where his friend's carriage is recognized.

The last of the stories published in the *American Monthly* was "P. Calamus."[37] It revealed that Willis could make himself and his editorial position the objects of good humor. P. Calamus is an editor of a weekly paper that in many respects resembles the *American Monthly*. The detailed description of the editor's paper-strewn office was sure to recall to readers Willis' own that he had given in previous editorials: "Some fifty unopened weeklys [*sic*], dailys, and other ephemera were tossed into one of its corners, a pair of scissors, some curiously cut and blotted scraps, and a pen redolent of unwiped antiquity, occupied the other, and in the centre stood the three necessities—inkstand, wafer, and sand box—clotted and sodden together by the sprinklings of innumerable inspirations":[38] the "curtail dog" asleep on the bad poetry recalls Willis' pet "L.E.L." The dramatic action of the story is the reception by P. Calamus of a *billet-doux* indicating an assignation with a lady at the Lamb Tavern. To pass the time until the meeting, the excited editor pitches into his work. Before the final scene, Willis pictorializes in liveliest fashion the interruptions to which an editor is subjected—one person with a news item; another with a whip and a threat because of an imagined insult; and, finally, a poetaster asking for an opinion of his work. Climactically, the editor goes to meet the lady. Literally, the end comes with death by emotional shock to the fifty-year-old bachelor.

These stories showed Willis' potential ability as a teller of tales. When he followed his own advice about brevity, he was most successful in constructing a narrative, as in "Miss Albina

McLush." Although his sentimental romances may have been successful with the ladies, one feels that he wrote this type of story because it was marketable. When he allowed his humor to break into a story and turned a joke upon a character who resembled the author, the resulting liveliness assured a better impression than that of the sentimental romances.

III   A Miscellany of Romances

In the romances which he wrote or adapted, Willis followed the formula of British and American tales popular with magazine readers of the time. There is, however, an unevenness in the quality of these stories. A few of the tightly constructed stories suggest that the author may have worked them over; others are discursive and excessively rambling. Arbitrarily, these romances might be divided into three types: (1) tales about people whom Willis had observed in a variety of situations and locales with which he was acquainted both in America and in Europe; (2) stories which he had read or heard about, and which he adapted for his audience; and (3) tales essentially Gothic in development.

Among the earlier stories which he chose to modify, many belonged to the romantic tale genre. A few of the altered romances appeared in *Inklings of Adventure,* a collection first published in England. "Baron von Raffleoff" became "Pedlar Karl." "Incidents in the Life of a Quiet Man" was changed to "Scenes of Fear," a more accurate but less ironic title. Parts of "A Morning in the Library" and "A Winter Scene in New England" were incorporated into a longer story, "Edith Linsey." And, finally, three stories were combined under the title "Larks on Vacation."

"Pedlar Karl" was as slight in plot as its predecessor. After his opening comments about Lebanon Springs as a summer resort, Willis developed the plot of the handsome European pedlar in search of his beloved Meeta. In the second version, he altered the story by having the character Phil Slingsby elope aboard a ship on the Hudson River. Unknowingly assisting Phil is his Aunt Isabel.[39]

Each story in "Scenes of Fear" is more tightly constructed than any of the rambling travel sketches, and in each he strove to achieve a particular effect. "The Disturbed Vigil" follows the earlier version closely. The narrator describes himself as having an extraordinary wakefulness and a taste for the macabre. There is horror in the scene where a white cat jumps upon the corpse of a young girl and raises the body upright with its fangs.[40] In the original story, the narrator is a student who simply aids his fellow students during their illnesses; in the later revision, the horror-addicted narrator has set down the unusual events in a journal. One passage reminds the reader of Poe's stories: "The sight of the long sheeted corpse, the sudden flare of lights as the long snuffs were removed from the candles, the stillness of the close-shuttered room, and my own predisposition to invest death with a supernatural interest, had raised my heart to my throat."[41]

In "The Mad Senior" Willis also concentrated macabre elements. Washington Greyling is pictured as a brilliant and courteous student who loses his reason from overwork. While the narrator maintains a night's vigil with the ill student, Greyling suddenly assaults him. The description is vivid, providing a final crescendo to contrast with the preliminary quiet tone in the narration of the preceding events.[42]

The third story, one which relied heavily upon the Gothic element, is effective in dramatic action. In "The Lunatic's Skate," Larry Wynn and the narrator have been friends since childhood. Willis employed autobiographical material in the story, for he makes a point as narrator to digress long enough to discuss the Unitarian beliefs of Larry's father, as compared to his own father's strict trinitarian beliefs. Willis justified the tangential material in the preface as evidence of the truth of the story. The climax of the plot occurs in a border town in the West. Larry has become a successful lawyer, as well as an active citizen in civic affairs. He plans his wedding; and the narrator, as an old and close friend, is to be best man. Larry, however, on the night of his marriage, under a lunar spell that repeatedly affects him when the moon is full, skates away into the freezing night on a nearby lake. An attempt at pursuit and rescue is unsuccessful, and the following day he is found frozen to death.[43] In this story, as in the two others, Willis gave specific names to his characters; this clearer identification had not been made in the earlier versions of the narratives.

The longer story, "Edith Linsey," was perhaps the most ambitious of Willis' short fiction. As the story was finally published, it was divided into four full-length chapters. Briefly, the plot concerns itself with Phil Slingsby's extended visit to the home of his friend Fred Fleming, his love affair with Edith Linsey who he believes is dying, her ultimate recovery with his help, and her final rejection of him.

Once again he incorporated earlier material. In the first chapter, "Frost and Flirtation," the details of a heavy snowstorm are ably written. The description is actually taken from "A Winter Scene in New England." So vividly did he picture the main characters on the point of being frozen to death that the dramatic suspense makes this part of the entire story the most successful. The narrative also includes part of an earlier paper that he had written upon subjects which were the favorites of Charles Lamb.

The second chapter, entitled "Love and Speculation," incorporated excerpts from the first version of "Minute Philosophies." These reflections, however, are presented in the story as excerpts from a family gazette that the Flemings write for their entertainment during the winter months. The second half of this same chapter is almost entirely sentimental in tone, depicting Phil and Edith in the Fleming library talking quietly with each other and awaiting her imminent death.[44]

Part III is frankly labeled a digression and included what is, in fact, a separate story in a lighter vein than that in which the longer story is told. Phil Slingsby acts the part of a John Alden. The transition to the main story was accomplished rather awkwardly: "I have no idea why I have digressed this time from the story which . . . I have not yet told. I can conceive easily how people who have nothing to do, betake themselves to autobiography—it is some pleasant rambling about over the past, and regathering only the flowers."[45]

Part IV finally brings the romance to a conclusion. Willis continued with recapitulations from his 1827 travelogue until his conscience called him back to the plot, at which point he rationalized: "The awkward thing in all story telling is transition. Invention you do not need if you have experience; for fact is stranger than fiction. A beginning in these days of startling abruptness is as simple as opening your mouth; and when you have once begun you can end whenever you like, and leave the sequel to the reader's imagination."[46]

The final scene conveniently situates Phil where he overhears Edith, who has completely recovered, telling one of the Fleming sisters about what was her temporary attachment to Phil. At their meeting shortly after, Phil tactfully ends their acquaintance by telling Edith the very reasons that she had expressed to her friend for ending their affair.

"Larks on Vacation" is composed of a trio of stories which had appeared in the *American Monthly Magazine*, including "Driving Stanhope Pro Tem" without change. The second story, an adaptation of "The Alias—Mr. St. John," was retitled "Saratoga Springs." Other changes were made in the plot. Phil Slingsby arrives at Saratoga with a severe sunburn. Later, in the disguise of a college senior and with his entire appearance improved, he meets and falls in love with Fanny Ellerton who had previously met Phil when he was unkempt and without disguise. Later in the story, as he resumes his own identity, Phil is left stranded by Miss Ellerton whose heart interests have changed.[47] The ending, less romantic than in the first version, is just as entertaining. The third story is the delightful "Mrs. Captain Thompson," included without any significant change.

Other stories which Willis identified as romances were "Niagara"; "Lake Ontario"; and "St. Lawrence," "Minute Philosophies"; "F. Smith"; "Incidents on the Hudson"; and "Tom Fane and I." In most of these stories too, he relied upon diary entries and earlier sketches.

"Niagara" reintroduces Job Smith. Willis interjected a slender story among many passages about the Falls. A short dramatic incident has Job serve as a human bridge to help a young lady to safety from a precarious rock.[48] In the second story of the group, "Lake Ontario," Phil Slingsby and Job continue to function as dramatis personae. Their banter about their trip and details about their entrance into Canada occupy the sketch. Left intact from the earlier pieces is the incident of a boy's pleading with an officer for his sister to return home instead of following her lover (a British soldier) to England.[49] Finally, in "St. Lawrence," the details of passage up the river are retained, but the story of an Indian girl following a man of the regiment who rejects her is new.

"Minute Philosophies," the title appropriated from an earlier essay,[50] tells the story of a man who teaches a young girl the beauties of external nature. The earlier piece was written in the style of Addison, but had the theme and subject matter of Wordsworth. In the second version, Willis took the elements of Wordsworth's nature philosophy from the earlier essay (which had appeared in the *American Monthly Magazine*) and incorporated them into the narrative. Typical of such passages is one which describes the mind in its first awareness of certain ideas: "Every topic seems to you like a phantom of your own mind from which a mist has suddenly melted. Every feature has a kind of half-familiarity, and you remember musing upon it for hours, till you gave up with impatient dissatisfaction."[51]

Another romance, "F. Smith," occupies the borderline between sketch and short story. Willis himself was not sure and humorously admitted: "I am not settled in my own mind whether this description of one of my favorite haunts in America [Nahant] was written most to introduce the story that is to follow, or the story to introduce the description."[52] Again, in this work, he used many autobiographical events, telling about his driving along a three-mile stretch of beach at Nahant behind his favorite horse Thalaba. The narrator confesses his penchant for reading, while in college, such works as the "Art of Love" rather than books on logarithms. The slight plot has Blanche Carroll, characterized as a "little devil," requiring Slingsby's friend Job to go to Salem on an errand and then to compose appropriate lines of poetry for her. Because of mistaken identity, Smith is thrown into the Lynn jail as a thief accused of having stolen "stanhope and bracelet." Released finally, through the help of Slingsby, Job forgives his scheming Blanche and composes his sentimental verses.

Two other romances in which Willis drew from personal experiences were "Incidents on the Hudson" and "Tom Fane and I." In the first, he narrated the varied events in a day of travel of tourists going on vacation, including a mistaken attempt at rescuing someone from drowning (the person overboard turns out to be a floating log) and an assault upon the Englishman in the party who is mistaken by a volatile Alabama man as making advances toward his sister.[53] Willis told the story in the manner of a society reporter and was successful both in his humor and brevity. "Tom Fane and I" is another example of the author's intermingling of romance and travel. The main scenes are at Saratoga, with the author's including appropriate apostrophes to the places of vacation rest. The action springs from a basic misinterpretation by one of the characters. Phil, in love with Kate Frump, believes that he overhears his friend Tom proposing to her; but Tom is actually making his addresses to Phil's sister. There follows the expected happy ending with Tom's helping Kate secure a fortune rightfully hers and Phil's marrying Kate.[54]

One story which is definitely in the Knickerbocker tradition and resembles the Hudson tales of Paulding and Irving is "Oonder-Hoofden," written to provide a legend for Undercliff, the home of George P. Morris, located near Cold Spring, New York.[55] Willis employed an historical setting for his tale and managed to stick to the main thread of his story. John Fleming, mate on Hendrick Hudson's ship *Half-Moon*, in anger fires upon and kills an Indian who he believes is stealing from the ship. After time has passed and friendly relations are apparently restored with the Indians, Fleming is lured ashore by a beautiful Indian girl. He believes that the death has been forgotten by members of the tribe, but he himself is killed at the hands of the Indian's widow. Willis produced an effective ending to the story: the tribe's chief and Hudson silently agree that justice has been reached.[56]

"The Picker and the Piler," another of the American stories, is remarkable for its unusual plot and surprise ending. The story begins in a small tavern in a sparsely settled area of frontier country. In this lumber region, the narrator meets a unique character who picks and piles the waste wood for the owner of the cleared lands. The reader discovers that the "picker and piler" enjoys his lonely occupation after his retirement from an adventurous life as a privateer on the sea. An unusual turn of plot is introduced. The owner of the land has seduced the picker's daughter. The story comes swiftly to a climax when the lumberman fells a pine upon the landowner.[57]

The American romances depended heavily upon the author's own experience transmuted through his diaries, his early story-telling, and his later reflections. Willis was successful when he exercised critical judgment and reduced the length of stories. His scene setting was also generally successful, for he had the ability of graphic description. But these stories revealed that, despite many good conclusions with elements of surprise for the readers, he was not able to handle structurally the longer short story.

IV *Adapter of Foreign Romances*

One of the results of travel abroad was Willis' composition of stories with foreign settings. Many of these tales were adaptations of romances which he had heard about or had read. Again, he followed the pattern of Irving, who had brought together such stories in the works which immediately followed the publication of the *Sketch Book*.

"The Gypsy of Sardis" is chief among those romances with their setting in foreign countries. This story is taken from material contained in letters which had appeared in 1834 and had been written from Smyrna and Constantinople. He again employed his narrator Phil Slingsby, who is accompanied by his old friend Job Clark. The romantic plot recalls the influence that Byron's Eastern tales, such as "The Bride of Abydos," may have had.

Introductory material retells the pleasures of American travelers on a picnic among the ruins of Sardis. The gypsy is the girl Maimuna who, on a trip to visit a relative, is seized by slavers for sale in Constantinople. The setting of the story allowed Willis to indulge in his descriptive powers by providing readers with impressionistic views of the minarets and mosques of this Eastern metropolis. Elements of both the mysterious and the exotic are given as he develops the plot with Maimuna as a prisoner of the Sultan.

Phil and Job attempt to rescue her by bribing their way into forbidden quarters with the help of the Sultan's perfumer whom they have befriended. Finally, they plan themselves to buy Maimuna in the slave market. After a few suspenseful interludes, they succeed in aiding the girl to freedom. Willis self-consciously admitted that he realized how a few of his digressions did interfere with the plot, but once again he rationalized that "life—real life—is made up of half-finished romance."[58]

A second story depending in part on a Near Eastern setting is "Widow by Brevet." Two American heiresses to a Salem business firm and their father entertain the son of a Turkish business associate. Hassan, the son, is not adept in speaking English, nor in writing it. After returning home, he sends a marriage proposal back to Salem. Interpreting the letter to mean her as the betrothed, the elder Miss Picklin sets sail for Constantinople. A plot complication is resolved when it is discovered at the story's end that, because of favorable winds, the second and younger Miss Picklin, whom Hassan had actually addressed, has reached Constantinople on a second ship ahead of the arrival of the older sister and has already married Hassan. The humorous tone of the story counterbalances Willis' straining credulity by his plot manipulation.[59]

Willis used Italy as the locale for many of these romances. "The Madhouse of Palermo," although unusual in subject matter, was also taken from a true-to-life experience: a visit to an asylum. In the story, a narrator visits a Count Pallagonia from whom he learns that all his servants are insane. He learns too the story of the Greek prince and his daughter, from a Sicilian count whose estate he visits. The count tells how he went through the form of marriage to aid the young princess regain her sanity.[60]

Other Italian romances may be found in the collections, *Inklings of Adventure* and *Loiterings of Travel*. A few had proven popular in the British magazine press and were printed in these collections and in later collections published in America during the 1850's. In this group are "Violanta Cesarini," "Pasquali, the Tailor of Venice," "The Revenge of Signor Basil," and "Paletto's Bride." Of all the stories, Willis believed that "Violanta Cesarini" should have been a novel.[61] He confessed toward the end of this romance: "You have ... in brief, what should have been well elaborated, embarassed with difficulties, relieved by digressions, tipped with moral and bound in two volumes."[62] A reader may well question whether or not there was enough material and substance for such a volume. In addition to Willis' complaint about the pressure of writing for periodicals, he did here, of course, ironically comment upon the standards of English publishers of the novel. He felt "sacrificed to the spirit of the age."[63]

The story is about Count Malespina and his daughter Violanta. The author tells about the history of the Cesarini families, the counts of this line having married out of their class by choosing peasant girls for their wives. The reader learns too that the Count's son is an outlaw and brigand. Other characters include the artist Biondo Amiero and his friend the artist Signor Giulio, a hunchback whom Violanta discovers is her brother and, therefore, heir to the Cesarini wealth. Sympathetically, she cultivates her brother's friendship and wins his confidence. The two plan a course of action to have him recognized as the rightful heir. A masquerade at the *Teatro della Pergola* brings a climax to the story. Violanta goes to the affair disguised as a hunchback and is made to appear as Giulio. The Count, her father, believes that she alone is wearing such a costume. By this evident ruse, Giulio gets the opportunity of speaking alone with his father and ultimately secures recognition as the rightful son.[64]

In "Pasquali, the Tailor of Venice," the title character and his wife plan to attend the festival of San Antonio in Venice. Although Fiametta, the wife, suffers from rheumatism, her husband insists that she accompany him in her light summer dress —the one in which she was married. The wife insists that their beautiful neighbor Turtarilla go with them. To avoid suspicion of his admiration for Turtarilla, Pasquali feigns protest at the suggestion. During the events Fiametta is accidentally soaked and, as a consequence, is so chilled that she becomes ill and is taken to a hospital. Not long after, through a perverse error of the hospital authorities, Fiametta's clothes are brought to the husband who believes that she is dead. He makes plans immediately to marry the comely Turtarilla, but is prevented at the altar from doing so when Fiametta reappears.[65] Although much of the story is highly contrived, it has the saving virtues of humor and tight construction.

Another Italian story, one which Willis often reprinted, was "The Revenge of Signor Basil." Signor Basil is a "designing villain," who meets and admires the Marchesa del Marmore while he is on board a steamer sailing from Venice. Later, quite by accident, he sees her in the cathedral in Bologna. There he accosts her, although she is attended by nobles of her coterie; and she grants him a perfunctory nod of recognition. This slight commences his "revenge." As the story develops, Count Basil is shown as a close confidant of the English lady

Geraldine in Florence. The third confrontation with the Marchesa occurs at the Tuscan Court, when Count Basil appears at a grand fête at the Pitti Palace in his full diplomatic regalia. The Marchesa becomes envious of his attentions to Geraldine. Ironically, as the Count's love for Geraldine grows, so does the love of the Marchesa for the Count. His joy, as Willis phrased it, keeps step with his revenge. Subsequently, Geraldine senses that she is being used as "a tool of revenge." Basil proceeds, when the opportunity offers itself, to humiliate the Marchesa. The surprise ending comes when the Marchesa finds comfort in the friendship of Lady Geraldine in England.[66]

In this story Willis again employed the elements of disguise and discovery. The story is different because of its ironic ending. Of relevance, but of secondary importance to the plot itself, is the picture of the artists in the early part of the story. For his setting, Willis relied upon his knowledge of Italian locations.

"Paletto's Bride," from *Loiterings,* touched only lightly upon a favorite theme, nobility in lowly circumstances. The locale is Venice, and the main actors are a father and his daughter. The reader learns through a conversation that a mysterious stranger has paid "particular and passionate attention to the daughter." The father pleads for her confidence, but later that same night she elopes with the "stranger" to whom she has been secretly married. She departs in a gondola rowed by Paletto who soon confesses his humble origin and abject circumstances. Before meeting Francesca, he had won at the gaming tables; using this money he had passed himself off as a noble. Recent losses, just before their escape together, had reduced him to the level of his former circumstances.

Willis shifts swiftly in time and in plot, and the reader next discovers that Count Fazelli has married Francesca. The story ends abruptly when it is found that the Venetian captain of the guard is Paletto. He comes to claim his wife Francesca, who has realized that she really loves him deeply. The romance is happily resolved with the dissolution of Francesca's second marriage. Since the plot was so obviously strained in construction, Willis hastened to assure his readers that he had heard the story in Venice.[67]

Another story with an Italian background was "Countess

Nyschreim and the Handsome Artist"; the scene is laid in the Pitti Palace where a young Scots painter, Graeme McDonald, works alongside a French paintress, Mlle. Jolie. The "hero" has been well described as "a spoiled child of genius."[68] As the result of a dare by one of his friends, Graeme paints the face of his fellow artist. Again Willis breaks the action in two parts; in the second half of the story, young McDonald receives a proposal by correspondence from a "Countess" who has heard of his abilities. Although he agrees to the marriage, he feels compelled to inform his bride-to-be that he is in love with a humble artist. McDonald goes to the church for the ceremony and finds a carnelian ring (which he had given to Mlle. Jolie) on the bride's finger, and he realizes that the fellow artist is the Countess. The characterization of McDonald is especially weak, for Willis did not convince his readers of any basis for his actions. Consequently, his weakness or lack of principle is inexplicable. Willis attempted an explanation of Graeme's complexity, but the letter that he has the Scotsman write accepting the marriage with qualifications is unconvincing.[69]

Two adventure stories, which appear quite obviously to be retellings of romances heard, are "My One Adventure as a Brigand" and "The Bandit of Austria." The narrator in the first story is accosted by an Englishman, St. John Elmslie, whom he had helped secure a place in a carriage to Geneva. At the inn at which the travelers stop for the night, the Englishman recognizes his wife from whom he had been separated. After a detailed explanation of the complications of his past marital life, St. John asks the narrator to help him by assuming the role of a brigand so that, in the excitement, he may elope with his own wife. The narrator performs his part to perfection, and the couple are reunited.[70]

Supposedly, the second adventure story was told the author by the Count D'Orsay. The romance consists of a series of exciting, although at times unexplained, incidents. It suffers, as do other stories, in having too much happen in too short a scope. The plot winds and twists through a duel which involves the narrator; the adventures of the narrator and his "noble" valet Percy; the pursuit of the Bandit of Austria, Yvain; his death by treachery; and ultimately the marriage of his widow to Percy.[71] The main characters are sketchily portrayed and lack adequate motivation. The story, it appears, was the receptacle of every device and technique of the romantic tale; it is so overloaded that it almost becomes a parody of the genre.

He next employed supernatural devices in both "A Revelation of a Previous Life" and "The Phantom Head upon the Table." The narrator within the first story is directly involved with a Lady Margaret to whom he seems to have the same voice as that of a young Viennese artist with whom she was once in love. She discovers that the narrator was born the very hour that her lover had died. Through his mysterious power of clairvoyance, the narrator senses the exact time the Lady Margaret dies.[72] Willis found it necessary in the story to explain the supernatural quality of the experience of the narrator—that of an individual losing a "sense of neighborhood," of becoming dissociated from his surroundings.

The second story is even less credible. Count Pallardos, a translator in the British Foreign Office, visits Aymar House on Berkeley Square. The socialite friends of the Lord pay no attention to the Count. However, he is reassured by the mirror that he has a nobility of "nature's lineaments." In a second episode, the Count borrows in Hyde Park an associate's horse so that he may ride by the side of Lady Aymar's carriage. In a final "chapter," Pallardos pays the Aymars a visit at what they consider a regrettable time, since it happens to be the day of the year on which Lord Aymar "sees" a phantom head. This specter is invisible to Lord Aymar's daughter, but it is seen by Count Pallardos. The event reveals the Count as the real child of the Lord.[73] As in a few of his early tales, Willis relied heavily upon the Gothic. These stories are less effectively written; consequently, readers cannot suspend their disbelief. The last tale about Count Pallardos is one of the author's weakest. Despite its weakness, however, the story was popular among British and American periodical readers.

Of no outstanding merit, and in the conventional romantic vein, were six other adaptations. Four had European settings: "Love and Diplomacy," "The Marquis in Petticoats," "The Wife Bequeathed and Resumed," and "The Belle of the Belfrey." Two Chinese stories which he retold were "The Poet and the Mandarin" and "The Inlet of Peach Blossoms."

The European tales all employ the disguise device. Count

Anatole in "Love and Diplomacy" becomes a valet in order to serve a Princess Leichstenfels with whom he is in love. The Marquis de la Chetardie in the second romance assumes a woman's role for King Louis XV of France to make necessary diplomatic contacts at the Russian Court.[74] The third tale is slightly more complicated in plot, but in "The Wife Bequeathed and Resumed" there is a May-December marriage between aging Count Montalembert and young Zelie. Before his contrived death, the count wills his title to a younger man, De Mornay, who has shown attention to Mme. Montalembert. When the new husband turns out to be an unfeeling rake bent upon humiliating his wife, the old count comes to life for a reunion with his wife. Actually, he had assumed the guise of a veteran soldier on his own estate.[75] Willis also used the disguise mechanism in "The Belle of the Belfrey." Mme. de Pomponney, having once been deceived in love, does not allow her pretty daughter Thenais out of her belfry room where they both live, particularly during the time the hussars stay in the town. She does allow Robertin, supposedly the village idiot, free visits to the daughter without suspecting him. Robertin, a hussar, does manage to take Thenais to a *fête-champêtre*. In the final unraveling of the story, Felix (alias Robertin) is found to be the son of Count de Brevanne's gardener instead of being the count's son. Mme. de Pomponney also reveals that Thenais is actually the count's daughter.[76]

Of all of Willis' work, "The Poet and the Mandarin" and "The Inlet of Peach Blossoms" are the least original. He made extensive but clever adaptations. The first story is quite stiff, stilted, and stylized. The poet Lepih enters a special garden at a celebration given by the Emperor Tang for his noble, Kwonfootse. Tang recognizes his poetic ability despite the objections of Kwonfootse. In the course of the story Lepih refuses an exalted rank and states that his wife will work for his own mother. This assertion is made with the knowledge that he is in love with Kwonfootse's daughter. Finally, Taya, the daughter, comes to Lepih's house. The theme must have had a special appeal to Willis because of its concern with natural versus artificial aristocracy.[77]

"The Inlet of Peach Blossoms," as Professor William Fenn has proved, is a sketch by Willis patched together from parts of Sir John Francis Davis' "The Poetry of the Chinese."[78] Willis did modify times, places, and names. The story is about Yuentssong's sparing of his enemy's life; his relationship with the beautiful Tehleen; the revolt of Szema, the enemy he had spared; and the ultimate death of both Tehleen and Szema.

The two Chinese tales reveal the weaknesses that exist in the other rewritten romances. When the action of a story is not based upon Willis' own experience, the artificial quality of the narrative becomes too evident. One senses that many of the romances were written with an eye to their immediate sale. Often, although characterization is weak, the scene-setting is successful, for Willis is then writing about what he has observed directly. The romances have too much action packed into too short a space; the characters act without plausible motivation. Willis was much more successful when he did not employ literary works as sole sources. When he modified his own life and lively experiences, the plots generally did not falter; and he succeeded in fusing theme, plot, and the other elements of his fiction.

CHAPTER 5

Sketcher of Society

I *Highlighter of High Life*

IN THE RANGE OF STORIES, one of the most significant
groups was that which dealt with society life in England and
in America. Although they are here separated from the sentimental tales, the sketches, the travelogues, and the romances, many
of these stories about society often have elements from these
other types. These tales of the *beau monde* include simple
romances without any social commentary, implied or stated;
humorous stories which have society life as the background;
short stories which primarily deal with the theme of nature's
nobility; and the novel *Paul Fane*. A few of the stories about
"high life" are presented with an American setting. For the
most part, all of the tales focus on contemporary life and
characters. This group includes "The Ghost Ball at Congress
Hall," "An Uptown Crisis," and "Count Pott's Stategy."

"The Ghost Ball at Congress Hall" is unusual in its combination of imagination and sentimentality.[1] Boniface, who works
at Congress Hall, imagines an after-season gathering of a
dream group; beautiful women who had stayed at the hotel
through many seasons return from times past. Willis was most
gracious in his depiction of these returning beauties. He succeeded in picturing the phantoms as real by his artful detail of
the events which transpire and by his characterization of Boniface, as he reacted to the events. Willis bridged time with
such a sentence as "The faces of the girls seemed to be those
of a past generation and their owners were in actuality
grandmothers."[2]

"An Uptown Crisis" characterizes parvenus in New York
society; the story has an ironical conclusion which appropriately

ends Willis' satire of a type. He makes fun of a Mrs. Leathers who aspires to acceptance by upper social groups. She calls in a Mr. Cyphers (the name is Dickensian) as her counselor on matters of taste and fashion. To a degree, Willis was making fun of his own avowed vocation as an arbiter of manners. Mrs. Leathers wishes to receive the grand duchess of local society. Part II supplies the irony, for the reader views "life in the basement." Mr. Leathers, a stockbroker, lives mostly below the stairs. Mr. Ingulphus, husband of the social queen, is revealed as being in financial straits and visits Mr. Leathers to ask him for credit. The intercession of Mr. Leathers' ward Lucy tilts in the most sentimental fashion the scales in favor of Mr. Ingulphus. He secures credit. When Mrs. Ingulphus visits Mrs. Leathers (above stairs) as recognition of her acceptance into society, the reader has been provided with one view of how parvenus succeed.[3]

"Count Pott's Strategy" recounts in detail the clever campaign waged by Mr. Chesterfield Potts for the hand of Miss Outhank. His social graces, his maneuverings, and departures are best identified by Willis as a "recipe for an approach" to successful courtship.[4]

The short stories which focus upon British high life vary in length and in quality. One of these which was often republished was "Lady Ravelgold's Romance."[5] The opening is fairly successful, but the descriptive ability which the author demonstrated in it was not sustained throughout the narration: "It was what was called by people on the continent a 'London day.' A thin, gray mist drizzled down through the smoke which darkened the long cavern of Fleet Street; the sidewalks were slippery and clammy; the drays slid from side to side on the greasy pavement, creating a perpetual clamor among the lighter carriages, with which they came in contact."[6]

The plot begins with the visit of Lady Ravelgold to the financial firm of Firkins and Company to secure a loan from the junior partner. She is represented by Willis, despite her aristocratic title, as a "fine specimen of Nature's nobility." The reader later discovers that she has helped the junior partner, a Mr. Tremlet, secure entrée cards to various social events. At many of these events he has had the opportunity of meeting Lady Ravelgold's daughter Lady Imogene and has formed an attachment for her. Before the resolution when Tremlet asks for Imogene's hand, Willis has given within the romance the detailed portraits of the ingenues at Almack's (an exclusive establishment catering to the members of British Society), as well as descriptions of the decor of the Belgrave quarters of Lady Ravelgold. Often he introduced within the story actual individuals with whom he had become acquainted during his stay in Britain. Ultimately, in the story Imogene reveals that she has found out that Tremlet is the natural son of a Count Manteuffel, after whose death he had been adopted by the English financier Firkins.[7]

In contrast to the length of "Lady Ravelgold's Romance" is "Lady Rachel." The story is narrated by a young man, Fleming, who is spurned by a member of the aristocracy. In his determination to overcome the aversion of Lady Rachel toward him, he becomes involved in a duel. The night before the duel is to take place, Lady Rachel (twenty years his senior) comes to him to confess her love. Having survived the duel with honor, Fleming receives word that Lady Rachel had declared herself only under the strength of the feeling that he would be killed the next morning.[8] Fleming's natural nobility is contrasted to her false actions. The shortness of the story did not allow the author adequate space for ample characterization so that the plot develops only in the most superficial manner.

In "Mr. and Mrs. Follett" Willis managed again an element of irony. As its subtitle indicates, it is concerned with the "dangers of meddling with married people."[9] The narrator plans to help his friend Tom regain his wife, who reportedly has had an alliance with a Count Hautenbras. Tom is started on the road to winning his wife back by the narrator's efforts. The approach is one to make the wife jealous. Mr. Follett ironically develops into "an incorrigible flirt."[10]

"Leaves from the Heart Book of Ernest Clay," in comparison with the other British tales, is altogether too discursive and rambling. Any reader feels immediately that too many of the "leaves" are missing. The narrator of the story, a friend of Ernest Clay, is an author writing for the *New Monthly Magazine*. On the way to pick up an advance from the periodical, Clay is stopped by a Lady Mildred, a close society friend. He, however, is in love with Eva Gore. At a party where he intends to show courtesies to Eva, an unfortunate chain of events pushes him into Mildred's company.

Willis, as if he were beginning another story at random, moves the reader to Florence where the story takes up Ernest's affection for a Julia whom he had met at a fête at the Pitti Palace. The story rambles on, detailing Ernest's trip through the Mediterranean area and his visit to the Naples studio of Ippolito Incontri, where he recognizes Julia's portrait as one of this artist's works. Ernest and Julia do not have any reconciliation of their relationship, and Ernest goes on to a love affair with Blanche Beaufin whom he marries. After her death, Willis presented a few more incidents in which Ernest is involved, but finally arranged the plot to have him reunited with Eva Gore.[11]

The entire story is incredible because of the deficiencies both in structure and characterization. The fact that Willis, who was capable of parody and irony, wrote the work seriously is regrettable. Situations which he employed here, in what truthfully appears as an abortive novel, he used with greater skill in *Paul Fane.*

A later story, but one related in a number of ways to the romances, is "The Icy Veil."[12] The title was derived from the mask of sociability assumed, and readily discarded, by the main character, Countess Isny Frere. In England, she leads the gay life of a "worlding," but has the reputation of being "proud, cautious, and passionless." The countess does confess to an artist (a Mr. Tremlet, the name borrowed from "Lady Ravelgold's Romance") that she leads two lives. In Germany, the countess retires to the privacy of a beautiful house where she gets away from the wearisomeness of the life of "well bred gayeties." Willis superimposed a romantic complication upon a simple plot. Tremlet becomes acquainted with a beautiful Tyrolese maid, Tessonda. At one point in the story, she envisions her aspirations accomplished imaginatively in a painting by the artist. Although Tremlet happily marries the countess, he becomes sad for the first time in his married life when Tessonda, who has had increasing success as a songstress, is unable to sing at Tremlet's house.

Such tales as these with an English setting do provide, to a degree, glimpses of British social life. The American pictures of society (discussed earlier in connection with Willis' American tales and in the succeeding section below) were handled more successfully. They are generally lively in presentation, since they are leavened with light humor and wit. Even the digressions of the British stories in which Willis often drew characterizations and background are not entertaining to a reader. In the shorter foreign pieces, but only in a few, the plots are tighter and, therefore, more plausible; but in them Willis failed to characterize successfully.

II *Humorist*

Willis' humorous stories are, in general, as slight as his other productions, but in them he never forgot the amusement of his readers. Politics and sentiment are intermixed in the right proportions in "The Power of an Injured Look."[13] Because of her husband's lack of attention, Mrs. Philip McRueit wears a pained expression on her face. When he realizes the negative political impact this injured look has on his fortunes, he changes his attitudes; she thrives; he succeeds.

Mr. G. is pictured in love with a widow in "Mrs. Passable Trott." They had been in love at twenty. After Mrs. Trott's husband dies, Mr. G.'s hopes for marriage revive; he sends his nephew as a go-between to the widow Trott. In a surprise ending, a twist to the plot, in which technique Willis anticipated O. Henry, Mrs. Trott marries the nephew who possesses all the desirable qualities Mr. G. had—at twenty.[14]

"Kate Crediford" parallels "Mrs. Passable Trott" in tone and is best summed up in a line from the story itself: "Flirtation is a circulating library in which we seldom ask twice for the same volume." The narrator sees Kate at the theater. He is concerned that she is unhappy in the partner who has escorted her there. Since he had dated her at one time, he writes a long letter expressing his concern. In return he receives a letter from Kate's husband indicating that she had been indisposed as a result of her having eaten unripe fruit.[15]

"The Female Ward," although it does not have a surprise ending, does have an unusual one. Once more the author employed the character of a first-person narrator. On an earlier trip Jem Thalimer and the narrator had befriended a Louisianian, Mr. Dauchy. When the two friends graduate from college, they are entrusted with the education of a young lady whom

Mr. Dauchy is sending North. There follow entertaining incidents revealing the frustrating search for lodgings in Boston by the two young men and the young lady. The respectability of their actions is continually questioned. The two finally succeed in finding a room in the back of Gallagher's Restaurant; but when Jem is criticized, they turn the young lady over to an insane asylum where she develops in both health and beauty.[16]

At the beginning of "Nora Mehidy," Willis chose to satirize himself and the difficulty of inspiration in story openings. He included three false starts as part of the story. Much of the story is mock serious in tone. When the story gets under way, the reader is introduced to the object of concern of Mr. Hypolet Leathers—the black locks of Nora Mehidy, daughter of a tailor. Through negotiation with the father, Mr. Leathers succeeds in buying the locks and subsequently has them made into a wig. The second half of the story continues Mr. Leathers' success; he gains the beautiful Nora in exchange for setting up Father Mehidy in a fashionable Broadway tailoring establishment.[17]

The real-life counterparts for the characters in "Those Ungrateful Blidgimses" Willis probably met among the American tourists who visited Florence. The parsimonious Blidgimses become a joke during one season among members of Florentine society. The narrator, unfortunately, because of a social obligation, has the job of chaperoning them on their European trip. When the two sisters fall ill in a coach on the way to Venice, he disguises himself as a sister of charity and subsequently administers them first aid. In disguise, he also functions as chambermaid. His ruse is discovered when the border police make a check of the carriage and its passengers, much to the embarrassment of the Blidgimses, whom the narrator humorously identifies as "ungrateful."[18]

In "The Spirit Love of 'Ione S.,'" the author singled out for ridicule many elements of sentimentality then in vogue in periodicals for women readers. He had, of course, inveighed against many of the more extreme stylistic devices of the sentimental schools of verse in the pages of the *American Monthly Magazine*. Willis set the contemporary background with his introduction: "Not long ago, but before poetry and pin-money were discovered to be cause and effect, Miss Phebe Jane Jones was one of the most charming contributors to a certain periodical

now gone over 'Lethe's wharf.' . . . Miss Jones abandoned authorship before the New Mirror was established, or she would,
doubtless, have been one of its paid contributors. . . ."[19]

The light approach is suggested in the characterization of
Miss Phebe Jones: "She was handsome as a prize heifer and
had a penchant for being melancholy."[20] Despite her assertions
about wanting to be "spirituelle," Gideon Flimmins is willing
to love her for her "outer inventory alone." She reads poetry
to him which she has written under the pen name "Ione S."
Phebe finally decides to find her soul-mate, whom she calls
"Ithuriel," by using the columns of the *Mirror*. She starts a poetical correspondence. A rendezvous is finally agreed upon. Rain
forces Phebe and her sister (who has accompanied her) to seek
shelter in an abandoned omnibus near the place of assignation.
Her spiritual "mate" comes to the bus too. A surprise and
delightfully humorous revelation occurs when a watchman's
light reveals her "Ithuriel" as the elder Flimmins, Gideon's
father. Willis closed: "Ione is not yet gone to the spirit-sphere
kept here partly by the strength of the fleshy fetter over which
she mourned, and partly by the dove-tailed duties consequent
upon annual Flimminses. Gideon loves her after the manner of
this world—but she sighs 'when she hears sweet music,' that her
better part is unappreciated—unfathomed—'cabined, cribbed,
confined'!"[21]

Although he employed humorous scenes within longer, more
serious stories, he did prove that he could compose short tales
wholly for the delight of his readers and write satirically by
turning the barbs toward himself and his own writing.

III   *Portrayer of Nature's Nobility*

The importance of a man's natural ability in balancing the
qualities of the aristocratic gentry is a theme which Willis repeatedly treated in short stories. Before the period of intensive
story writing, he had adapted his travel essay "St. Lawrence"
by picturing the nobility of an Indian girl who had devoted
herself to a British soldier. Willis favored the girl in his treatment, so that readers would be sympathetic toward her.[22] Another tale which re-echoes this theme is "The Cherokee's
Threat."[23] The author's digression is placed early in the story.

He rhapsodizes upon the similarities of a college community to a republic. Before the reader gets to the main action, he must also read the writer's praises for New Haven as a "metropolis of education." The central character, St. John, is an exceptional student whose room is furnished in the latest decor. The heroine of the sketch, however, is Nunu, daughter of a Cherokee chief, who resides at Miss Ilfrington's School for Young Ladies. It becomes apparent that, as St. John joins the young ladies in their daily constitutional, he and the young princess have met before. When a young Georgian miss plays the coquette with St. John, Nunu, feeling rejected and hurt, swings herself over a precipice, while grasping a tree limb, and threatens death unless she is recognized.

The author makes a transition to a date five years later, and readers have a glimpse of Nunu and St. John among a group of chiefs returning home from Washington. St. John confesses to the narrator: "I have ransacked civilized life to the bottom and found it a heap of unredeemed falsehoods." He ends by contrasting Nunu whom he praises with the "dolls of civilization."

An unusual story in which the scenes alternate between England and America is "Wigwam vs. Almack's."[24] Here the author used once again a narrator who tells the story, or retells what he hears about the characters. The narrator stops at Athens, a small village in the Pennsylvania wilds. The daughter of the village innkeeper, Ruth Plymton (who has recently been left an inheritance), is overheard talking to Shahatan, a local Indian chief, expressing her love for him, but seriously discussing with him all the possible objections to their marriage. Later, Willis introduced as part of the plot development an extract from a New Orleans newspaper telling of Shahatan's graduation from an Eastern college with academic honors. Willis provided his readers with a picture of a "banquette at an Almack's ball" as well as gratuitous comments on the natural aristocracy. After making a few pertinent remarks about aristocratic beauty in England, he focused attention upon a metamorphosed Ruth.[25]

The narrator visits Ruth in her Grosvenor Place home; and, during the conversation, she defines what she considers luxury, which in the light of the author's repeated concern with aristocracy, fashion, and "nobility" in poverty or in lowly station has a particular relevance within the framework of the story. She calls it the "science of keeping up the zest of the senses rather than pampering them." Willis introduced another narrator, a Mrs. Mellicent, to report upon what happens to Ruth. Actually, a short, short story is introduced within the longer tale. Mrs. Mellicent and Ruth succeed in confusing a fortune seeker who is never quite sure whether Ruth or Mrs. Mellicent is the heiress. Once again before the story ends, the author shifted scene and narrator. The narrator is visited in his Susquehennah home by an Englishman who had been traveling in the West. He tells of having met Shahatan in an Indian village which was a "primitive Arcadia." Ruth, having become disgusted with London, has chosen to live in the wilderness with one of nature's noblemen.[26]

In four other American stories, Willis gave his readers variations upon this theme of natural ability: "Born to Love Pigs and Chickens," "Two Buckets in a Well," "Mabel Wynne," and "Meena Dimity." Ephraim Bracely is the representative natural gentleman in the first story. On a visit to New York City, his fiancée reveals herself as aspiring to enter fashionable life. A friend of Meg Pifflit (the fiancée), a Miss Julia Hampson, takes advantage of an invitation to visit the Pifflit farm. It is anticipated by Ephraim and Meg that the city woman will be extremely snobbish. On the contrary, she reveals herself to be a woman who loves farm life and who realizes Ephraim's worth as an individual. She becomes Mrs. Bracely; Meg finds herself a city husband; readers had their happy ending.[27]

In "Two Buckets in a Well," Fanny Bellairs urges her lover to seek a commercial career rather than become an artist. She would be affluent, she avers, before she would be artistic. Philip, the fiancé, promises to follow her advice. He goes abroad, succeeds in his commercial endeavors, and returns a mature, sophisticated, well-dressed gentleman. Expecting to marry him, Miss Bellairs holds a fête at the cottage she has prepared for his homecoming and their marriage. When he views these things, he leaves; he has realized finally how much he has lost in the years he has been away while following a career which was really not the one in which he was happy.[28]

Two other American variants on nature's nobility theme are

found in "Mabel Wynne" and "Meena Dimity." The first story narrates the competition of two suitors, Mr. Blythe and Mr. Bell-allure, for the hand of Mabel Wynne, "the top most sparkle on the crest of the first wave of luxury that swept over New York."[29] She learns that she has inspired one of the two men to raise himself socially from a lowly station. Mr. Blythe, she is told, is from a good family; Mr. Bellallure is sartorially excellent. She has difficulty making up her mind which is the truer. When her father loses money, Bellallure is revealed as the fortune seeker.[30]

"Meena Dimity" satirizes false aristocrats. Brown Crash woos both the aristocratic Harriet Dyapers and the less fortunate Meena. Crash at first is intrigued by the Dyapers' wealth; but, when he feels that Harriet's attitude is condescending and that Meena has been snubbed, he becomes betrothed to Miss Dimity and declares his republican beliefs.[31]

Willis also wrote stories with a British setting that are concerned with the same theme. In his tale of English society, "Beauty and the Beast," he employed an English artist as narrator. The plot involves a Mrs. Titten, who commissions the artist to paint a literal likeness of her extremely ugly husband and then to do one in which he is idealized. Finally, as a third requirement, she asks the artist to paint a picture of Mr. Titten in fancy dress. The storyteller reveals later that the "ugly" picture is "spotlighted" in a prominent place in the Titten home; the idealized portrait is placed in the boudoir. Here Willis' rather obvious symbolism emphasized the theme of innate nobility, and the corollary that people with basic good qualities, regardless of exterior ugliness, care little for the world's opinion.[32]

"Brown's Day at the Mimpsons" has for its main character one very much like Ernest Clay. The narrator characterizes Brown as a "mirror of vulgarity," depending upon the circumstances. As a lark, Brown reaches at random for a letter of introduction which is five years old and which he had never used. He manages to be invited to the Mimpsons (to whom the letter is addressed) as a business associate of Mr. Mimpson. At their house, he finds that Mrs. Mimpson is sponsoring a friend who is to "come out" in society at Almack's. Brown secures tickets for the exclusive social affair after he has been snubbed by Mrs. Mimpson. Petulantly, he gives the tickets to a Miss

Bellamy and secures social revenge against Mrs. Mimpson. Although Willis makes a point about the pretensions of those aspiring to social station, he may have lost the sympathy of readers.[33]

Taking his point of departure from the 1832 journal, Willis told the story of "Light Vervain," which anticipated part of the plot of *Paul Fane*. In the short tale, the Skyrings in society have refused the company of artist F——. Finally, he is in a position where he can help Mr. Skyring for the sake of the daughter Kate. In thanks for his aid, however, he is criticized for seeming patronizing. F—— returns to the States, but as a painter he is not inspired until he receives a letter from Kate proposing marriage and restoring his confidence in his natural abilities.[34]

Perhaps the most successful story dramatically and thematically of this group is "Miss Jones' Son," which treats humorously of a Sir Humphrey Fencher's patronizing of a young man he remembers only as the son of a former servant, Miss Jones. James S., the son, actually has a reputation as a great wit in social circles. In the course of the story, he visits his mother while he is en route to Warwickshire. His mother volunteers to write a letter of introduction for him to one of her early admirers, Sir Humphrey Fencher, who happens to live near his destination in Warwickshire. Sir Humphrey and his family receive James S. only as "Mr. Jones," and he allows himself to fall into the role. The plot is humorously complicated by the Fenchers' talking about James S. and his expected arrival at the mansion of a Lord Beaufort. Patronizingly, Sir Humphrey makes arrangements for Mr. Jones to view the affair from the servants' area. The delightful ending has the Fencher family disappearing rapidly after Jones' appearance as James S.[35]

In choosing to develop the theme of natural aristocracy, Willis extended the area covered by his "studies of manners." He was successful in those stories where he adhered as a conscious artist to the principle of brevity and in which he combined the shorter structure with controlled wit and satire. In a few stories, his use of the surprise ending contributed to the entertainment of the works. In his treatment of a segment of American and British society, he extended the subject matter of American short fiction to new fields. He was to extend this boundary further with his writing of a full-length fictional work on manners.

IV Forerunner of the "International" Novel

Certainly, the most ambitious of Willis' fictional efforts was *Paul Fane*, written in 1856 and published the following year. He had complained that the pressures of writing for the periodical press prevented the writing of a longer work. He finally found the time to compose a novel when there was some abatement from the pressures of editing and writing articles. Repeated in the novel are many characterizations which he had earlier written in sketches and other shorter pieces. Many stories such as "Light Vervain" had focused upon an American artist. Others sounded the theme of natural nobility. Recurring in the plots was the device of disguise. Willis combined these elements, and others, in the novel. He admitted, moreover, that much of the subject matter was autobiographical.

The novel takes place after the summer of 1850. Paul Fane attends college because his father wishes him to prepare for the ministry; but the young man, who has an "unconquerable passion" for art, secretly studies it. His mother, knowing his secret, often discusses with him what he has learned.

At the home of his friend Phil Cleverly, Paul meets Mildred Ashly, an event which is to change "the whole current of his life." His reaction to her is unusual: ". . . she had become a creature of intense interest for him, but it was no beginning ever so remote, of a passion. There was more distaste than love in his sentiment towards her."[36] Paul had invariably been a favorite in any society with which he associated; and when Mildred Ashly looks upon him *"with no recognition of him as an equal,"*[37] Paul wonders what might be the "impassable chasm" between him and a "group who by blood have inherited accumulated culture and refinement through generations."[38]

Although his interest in art had first drawn him to traveling and studying in Europe, Mildred's attitude influences his decision to go—to study art and to search for the answers to questions about his position as an individual in society. Before his departure he seeks the advice of Mary Evenden with whom he had grown up. She knows only of his abiding interest in art, and her comment about studying abroad anticipates a character in Henry James' story, "The Madonna of the Future": "I am so glad you give up, at last, that misplaced Americanism of trying to be an artist here. You need the air of Italy—the collision with other schools of artists."[39] Finally, Paul becomes in Florence a fellow artist of Wabash Blivins, whom he had known in college and with whom he shares an old Palazzo studio. There they employ the same model, Giuletta.

Before his arrival in Italy Paul had secured an appointment to the American legation in Paris; consequently, he has no trouble gaining entrance to the Florentine Court. Among his new friends are the Palefords, a retired colonel and his daughter Sybil. Willis chooses to construct parallel plots; and, as he unfolds the story of Paul, he devotes chapters and parts of chapters to 'Bash. He becomes a frequenter at the Firkins' palazzo, for he is particularly interested in 'Phia Firkins, an heiress of an American family with business interests in Florence.

Another friend whom Paul first meets at a ducal fête is a princess. From the very first he has a high regard for her, thinking of her as an "eagle born among sparrows of society."[40] As he comes to know her, he finds that her natural instinct of superiority is manifest in her intellect. In a long conversation, she indicates how desirous she is of knowing men "who are particularly gifted by nature." She analyzes in an almost Jamesian tone: "There is something without language, Mr. Fane, which tells how we seem to others and it degrades us to be admired by some minds—they so vulgarize and materialize all they look upon."[41] She comes to assume the role of his confidante; she reveals herself, too, as a sculptress and among artists has hidden her identity as a princess. The two spend much time examining and talking about her art work. Paul finds a second friend in an Englishman, Mr. Tetherly.[42]

Paul's sensitivity about being looked down upon returns when he is asked by Sybil Paleford to escort a Mr. Ashly to her home. Paul recalls instantly the slight he had earlier received from Ashly's sister. Ashly has what appears to be the same disdainful attitude toward others. Paul is gratified later, ironically enough, when he hears that Ashly had made favorable comments about Paul's art work but had not known the identity of the creator.

The complexity of the story increases when Winifred Ashly, Mildred's sister, comes to Florence to sit for her picture after the other members of the family have departed for England.[43] Paul offers to do her portrait but disguises himself as a "Mr.

Evenden." While she is in Florence, Winifred, after being infatuated with Paul, meets his friend Tetherly; the two find each other temperamentally suited and marry.

Irony is introduced when Paul, who convinces himself that he is in love with Sybil Paleford, is asked by Mildred Ashly to help her in winning Sybil for her brother.[44] He decides he can best help Sybil by doing a picture of the brother, spiritualizing his good qualities on canvas. After finishing Arthur Ashly's portrait, Paul delivers the picture to Sybil and reveals the identity of the artist to Mildred who once again appears to draw the line of position between herself and Paul, despite the fact that she has praised his work unknowingly.

Willis provides both a happy and hopeful ending. Sybil is married to Arthur Ashly; Paul finally leaves Italy for England. Catherine Kumletts, friend of 'Bash Blivins' 'Phia, visits England; and Paul thus has the opportunity of reading what 'Phia has written about him. He is enabled finally to perceive that there are two sides to his character. In England, he sees both Sybil and Mildred once more. Although working busily, he determines to return to America. The princess, who urges him to stay in Europe, writes regarding America: "There are great elements maturing under the rough surface . . . a great seed germinating among the weeds which America has had no time as yet to eradicate."[45] And she finally advises that Mary Evenden is ready for love.

Because he has achieved recognition in England, Paul feels it is time to depart. He observes however: "I began where I never could have reached by my own merit only." As he further phrases it, he wants "to be appreciated below his present level": "Whatever might have been their [the British social groups'] decision, if you could have applied to it without influence or favor, it is inseparable from illusion. . . . They believe in you by recommendation of higher authority than their own judgment."[46] Paul is further satisfied that he can pick out nature's nobility from among the middle class and that the "hell of social life, and of all life, is false position." Finally, Willis had Paul express his hope for the future: "Though I know I have improved in the knowledge and dexterities of Art, while abroad, I wait till I get home for the inspiration to conceive what shall be only my own, and achieve in it a triumph."[47]

To anyone who had first studied themes, subject matters, characterizations, and locales in his earlier fiction, *Paul Fane* came as no shock. He had treated in so many stories the American artist, writer, or gentleman in European society, or the young man spurned by those of higher social standing. And events in the early pages of the novel parallel events in his life. His father had been hopeful that he would enter the ministry, while the son had increasingly devoted himself to belles-lettres.

The description of Paul in the novel offers a portrait of Willis which has been confirmed by the reminiscences of his Yale classmates. Willis did pass life "in a circle of very vague social distinctions." He offers a fairly keen insight into his own personality by this fictionalized projection. Paul, he wrote, is a man "with personal presence and manners better than his family circumstances...."[48] He continued: "[He has] a nature of large hope and confidence, and unusually quick tact and adaptability, he had been everywhere an unquestioned favorite, and the possibility of a society to which he could not be promptly welcomed, or in which he should not find it easy to please had never occurred to him."[49]

Certain situations in the novel inevitably call to mind the work of other authors—the style of Dickens, Thackeray, and Eliot. At other times, he anticipates James. The unity of *Paul Fane* is spoiled by the introduction of chapters about 'Bash, a character who does, however, provide notes of comic relief to an otherwise serious narrative. In almost Dickensian incidents, Willis has 'Bash visit the Firkins' palazzo. He pictures the wealthy Miss Firkins attracting many members of the nobility. Reminiscent of Dickens and Thackeray are such characters as Lady Highsnake, Sir Cummit Strong, and Count Ebehog.

As George Eliot and later Henry James would do, Willis attempted to explain how slight events within a story sometimes have important consequences. For example, at a ducal fête, when the Grand Duke himself asks Sybil to dance, Paul at this very moment meets the princess. Willis underlined the event as unstartling in itself, but one which actually has a bearing later upon the events in the young man's life.[50] The scene in which the princess discusses how so many people vulgarize recalls for the modern reader one of James' late short stories, "The Velvet Glove." James dealt with this same question of vulgarization. Oddly, the vulgar admirer in James' story is a princess who, to extend her fame as a rather less than mediocre novelist, flatters an American writer lionized by English society. Of course, in Willis' work a rapport is established between Paul and the princess, a relationship which in itself again recalls extensive use of main character and confidante.

As Professor Wegelin has indicated, Willis was among those pre-Jamesian writers of the nineteenth century who "felt the need to define their own and their country's relation to Europe." He might even be credited with trying to secure recognition of "cosmopolitanism" as part of American life, not only through the themes which he treated in his short fiction but also through his editorial writing for the periodicals.

In his fiction he tried, but never quite succeeded, in getting far below the surface of a character as James did later in the century. Because he was not the technical master of the art of the novel, as James was, one must finally admit to his sensitivity as an author but see him as one not able to give readers a meaningful insight into the ambivalence of characters.

The significance of manners did concern him as it later concerned James. Knowing his audience, Willis was well aware of their interest in European high life. As Wegelin indicates, "In story after story the heartless snobbery of fashionable European society is his theme; again and again one of nature's noblemen proves his superiority over the artificial social distinctions of Europe."[51] Professor Wegelin establishes Willis' position as an early writer of the international novel: "Willis was exceptional in being motivated by an almost exclusively social interest in Europe."[52] He summarizes to what degree *Paul Fane* anticipated James' early motifs.

V *Professional Storyteller*

Willis continued as a teller of tales for thirty years, from the time of his publication of a story in the *Legendary* until the printing of *Paul Fane* in 1857. Adapting the fictionalized sketch from Irving, he dealt with similar subject matters but ranged beyond into new fields. His travelogue-short stories, especially those published in the *American Monthly Magazine,* most closely resembled Irving. However, having early in his career expressed a wish to write about society, he turned to this subject in many of his shorter works. He was concerned in them and in his travel essays with setting down impressions of the passing human show. Often delightfully amused by what he saw, he attempted to convey graphically what he experienced in such a manner as to entertain his readers.

Negatively critical of the circumstances which "forced" him to compose shorter works, he nevertheless sensed the appeal of briefer stories to his reading audience. He was perhaps most successful when he used the third-person and set down events simply and chronologically. His use of a fictional narrator such as Phil Slingsby was also successful, although the story within Phil's frame of reference was told in the first person. Having gained experience in writing chatty, discursive editorials, he unfortunately at times carried over this rambling tone into stories. These tangential sections are sometimes delightfully written, but often interrupt the tale

From the beginning of his career, Willis had a remarkable talent for employing his experiences in his stories. Although not so adept as Henry James came to be, he did find a fictional formula—similar to that used by the later author—of interweaving travel experiences with the fictional plot. There is a freshness in his sketches which derives from an ability to convey enthusiasm and excitement about people and places. He used his diaries to good advantage, but his keen memory and vivid imagination shaped the presentation of the story.

When Willis followed popular taste and adhered to the framework and subjects of the traditional sentimental tale, he did not succeed. This failure is especially true of his adaptations, his retelling the stories of others. When he did not draw upon his own experience, he did not have the ability to transmute the tale into something his own. When he worked at achieving a single effect in a story, he was frequently an able author. Such stories as "Kate Crediford," "The Female Ward," and "Mrs. Passable Trott" show how he could do this with humorous intent. In his more successful Gothic tales, as in "Scenes of Fear," he established well a single atmosphere of terror.

He was conscious of the weakness of sentimental romances

which relied upon an excessively emotional treatment of a subject. He was guilty of such sentimentality in "The Death of the Gentle Usher," but he was able to satirize or parody the style in a story like "The Spirit Love of 'Ione S.'" As with parody or satire, he was often successful when he dealt with humorous situations in which he placed as the butt of the joke a character such as Phil Slingsby, who closely resembled himself.

Willis made definite contributions to the development of the short story in his treatment of English high life and American fashionable life. In these tales he was on surest ground when he told lightly and humorously of events, situations, and characters. When he satirized gently and when he commented wittily, his stories contained a liveliness that his serious romances did not.

It is true that there was in Willis, as there had been in Cooper, an ambivalence in attitude—the combination of admiration for aristocratic manners and the dislike of caste. Willis did not resolve the enigma in his fiction; he approached solutions. In many essays written in the 1850's, after he had ceased for the most part to write shorter fictions, he expressed the hope that there would develop an American cosmopolitanism brought about by the junction of the "pocket" aristocracy and the artistic one. He had an awareness of his American public and its attitudes, which were also characterized by an ambivalence. Representative readers would probably deprecate the man "who would be intellectually better than the mass" at the same time that they aspired to better their social station or position.

One might finally reiterate, then, that any cursory examination of the entire body of Willis' stories reveals that he excelled in passages of impressionistic description, in witty phrasing, in the use of a fairly good sense of dramatic incident, and in his attention to and fictional treatment of certain themes not previously dealt with by American writers.

CHAPTER 6

Versatile Littérateur

I Sentimental Versifier

"VERSATILE" and "prolific" are the adjectives which best describe Willis' production as a writer during more than forty years as an author. Although his reputation in American literary history may be firmly established upon his abilities as a short-story writer, an essayist, and as a magazinist, his other literary productions should not go unrecognized; for many have merit.

His verses gave him a "national reputation" before he was out of his 'teens. He continued to write poems throughout his life, although he wrote fewer in his later years. In addition to his accomplishments in versifying, he was a creditable playwright. In the late 1830's, two plays which have been preserved, *Tortesa* and *Bianca Visconti*, were stage successes. They equal in dramatic merit the romantic dramas of the time, such as those written by Robert Montgomery Bird.

Willis also performed another literary function in collaboration with his fellow editor of the *Mirror*, George Pope Morris. Willis as an editor of anthologies became a purveyor of culture. He selected works of many contemporary authors of America and Europe for these editions. All the journals of which he was coeditor—the *New York Mirror*, the *New Mirror*, the *Evening* and the *Weekly Mirrors*, and the *Home Journal*—were literary journals including on their pages many poems. His recurrent editorial statements underlined the belletristic aim of the two Knickerbocker magazinists. Like Morris, Willis earned a wide reputation as a versifier. His career as a poet actually began while he was still an Andover student. According to his biographer Beers, he sent verses to his sister as early as 1823.

His father encouraged the son's versifying by printing his work in the *Boston Recorder*. Before his graduation from Yale, Willis had also contributed to the *Christian Examiner*, the *Memorial*, and the *Connecticut Journal*. In 1826 a committee for the *Boston Recorder* had awarded him a prize for the poem "The Sacrifice of Abraham."[1] He had secured his reputation in 1827 by winning a $50 prize for verses submitted to the *Album* and another prize for "Absalom" (another scriptural adaptation). While he was editor of the *American Monthly Magazine*, he published many of his poems. By the year he first became editor, he had already published two volumes of poems, *Sketches* and *Fugitive Pieces*, appearing in 1827 and in 1829, respectively.

After the poems of his college days, it was natural that inspiration for many poems derived from his travels and from significant personal events. Because of his increasing magazine reputation in the 1830's and 1840's, fellow editors often pirated his poems.

It was Willis' practice, when a volume of his verse appeared, to reprint in later editions much of his earlier work. The 1837 volume, *Melanie and Other Poems*, included "The Dying Alchymist," "The Leper," "Parrhasius," "The Wife's Appeal," and "The Scholar of Thebat ben Khorat"—all of which he had published in the *American Monthly Magazine*. This same procedure was employed in the edition of *Sacred Poems*, published as a supplement to the *New Mirror* in 1843. In prefatory remarks, Willis justified republication by indicating that the subjects of these verses "have given them a popularity independent of criticism."[2] The same was true of *Poems of Passion*, also published the same year. The pattern was repeated three times in 1845, 1850, and 1865: in the volumes *Poems, Sacred, Passionate, and Humorous* (1845), *Poems of Early and After Years* (1850), and in the latest edition.

Before an examination of representative selections from his poetry, it is important to recall, as any review of the *American Monthly Magazine* would give evidence, that he was well acquainted with the English poets from the Elizabethan era through the early nineteenth century. His reviews and editorials revealed an extensive acquaintance with the British romantics who were his contemporaries and who often influenced him. He was as well alert to public taste regarding poetry. For example, in July, 1830, Willis indicated the dearth of poets in America: "If poetry were not the very breadth and pulsation of some hearts, there would be no such thing in our country. As a branch of literature, it is not at all followed, now."[3]

In an early review for the *Token* of 1830, he expressed regret about the "lack of good poetry writing." Too often men of talent were so rebuked by irresponsible critics that the would-be versifiers left the field entirely. Yet he had hope for the future: "the age of poetry is not gone."[4] He had words of encouragement for the young poet, indicating the wide number of sources of poetry in nature's marvels, in past times, and in "human thoughts and affections." While admitting the faults into which young writers often fall, Willis felt that, if the younger men and women would exercise greater "severity of taste," they would come to reject the ornamental. In an article the following month, he expressed his opinion that the new schools of poetry were limited to "the sentimental and the metaphysical." He concluded: "now the mind with all its gifts, and the heart with all its hidden feelings are the only themes read or written on."[5]

In December, 1829, he spoke of the lack of adequate remuneration for men who wanted to write.[6] Almost thirty years later in 1856 in the volume *Rural Letters,* he reprinted his "letter to a young poet" in which he described in great detail the "condition of American authors who have to stay in other professions because of atrocious copyright laws."[7] Willis was realistic in describing the great trouble it was for anyone to acquire position, reputation, and fame in literature. Previously, in 1829, he had indicated that the reading public often labeled a poet as having a "suspicious reputation." Poetry was looked upon by many as an "innocent weakness" cured by age. While conceding in another review that truthful criticism was welcome, he felt that critics should not condemn poets in order to spice their articles, nor for that matter "freeze the unhappy writer with faint praise for qualities he did not possess...."[8]

He was quite open in his attack on extremes in styles and subjects of the versifiers: "We are as much an enemy of sentimentality of writing as any one. We have been as much annoyed by boarding school poetry, and lack-a-daisical prettyisms. But we dislike equally the morbid depravity of taste, which craves only a constant and unnatural excitement."[9] In his own poetry, Willis did not transcend the trends of his times; he followed the conventions of the eighteenth- and nineteenth-century romantic schools of poetry. Although he was generally sincere in his poetic expressions and in his choice of themes when he wrote about events in his personal life, he did often follow current tastes in sentimentality; for he knew well the readers of the periodicals for which he wrote.

Throughout his life, he was devoted to Byron's cause; and he emulated his work. The English poet often exercised a significant influence. In early poems, such as "Misanthropic Musings"[10] and the work beginning "My childhood has been happy, Yet/I had some hours of shadowed thought,"[11] Byron's influence can be noted. William Ellery Leonard in *Byron and Byronism in America* has stated that the most complete imitation of the British author's "Tales" was in Willis' *Melanie* which appeared in 1837.[12] The narrator within the story, Rodolph de Brevern's son, is Byronic in temperament. His deep melancholy is characterized in such lines as "Life had no joy, and scarce a pain,/Whose wells I had not tasted deep."[13]

The son of de Brevern and his sister travel to Italy where in the course of the story she falls in love with a young painter, Angelo. The brother is envious of his sister's devotion to the young man, but finally accepts the situation. When the sister is about to marry him, a nun watching the ceremony reveals herself as Angelo's mother; the bridegroom is Melanie's half-brother. In the tale, Willis purveys the "Byronic dark and terrible in love and crime."[14] The setting, the tone, and the human relationships of the main characters are all Byronic, recalling elements of such works as "The Bride of Abydos," and "Manfred."

In the collected poems, there are many verses which reflect the older poet's influence. Among these are poems dealing with the subject of separated lovers: "To Ermengarde," "The Confessional," "She Was not There," "Fail Me Not Thou," and "Despondency in Spring."[15] There are passages in "The Confessional" and "Florence Gray," resembling works of Byron, that employ the experience of European travel: "I thought of thee—I thought of thee/Where glide the Bosphor's lovely waters,/All palace lined from sea to sea,"[16] or from "Florence Gray":

> I was in Greece. It was the hour of noon
> And the Egean wind had dropped asleep
> Upon Hymettus, and the thymy isles
> Of Salamis and Egina lay hung
> Like clouds upon the bright and
>   breathless sea.[17]

Leonard also has indicated that Willis' longer poem "Lady Jane" imitated elements of Byron's social and literary satire found in "English Bards and Scotch Reviewers" and in *Don Juan*. Willis' poem uses the same *ottava rima* metrical stanza which Byron so successfully employed in *Don Juan*. There is in both works the same straining humorously for rhyme. Willis opens:

> There was a lady—fair, and forty too.
>   There was a youth of scarcely two and twenty.
> The story of this love is strange, yet true.
>   I'll tell it you. Romances are so plenty
> In prose, that you'll be glad of something new,
>   And so I'll versify what did and meant he.
> You think he was too young!—but tell me whether
> The moth and humming-bird grow old together![18]

As Byron often made reference to contemporary writers, so does Willis. Allusion is made in the work to Barry Cornwall, Moore, Landor, Bulwer, Bowring, Disraeli, and Joanna Baillie. More than once Willis has fun at Byron's expense:

> Some men, 'tis said, prefer a woman fat—
>   Lord Byron did. Some like her very spare.[19]

Or:

> Byron was a man and bard, and Lady B.
>   In wishing to monopolize him wholly
> Committed bigamy, you plainly see.
>   She being very single, Guiciolli
> Took off the odd one of the wedded three.[20]

In *Lady Jane*, Willis satirized the fact that, under certain conditions, anyone could become an author. He also ridiculed the uses made of social acquaintances. He may well have had

Lady Blessington and her entourage in mind when he commented upon Countess Pasibleu's suite:

> The Countess Pasibleu's gay rooms were full,
>   Not crowded. It was neither rout nor ball
> Only "her Friday night." The air was cool;
>   And there were people in the house of all
> Varieties, except the pure John Bull.
>   The number of young ladies, too, was small—
> You seldom find *old* John, or his *young* daughters,
> Swimming in very literary waters.[21]

Willis was successful in achieving Byron's casualness of digression, as well as a "conversational facility" in the stanzas.

Willis was no innovator, and it does him no discredit that his talents were mainly derivative. His abilities were those of an adapter and of a composer of competent metrical lines. In regard to form, he did employ a variety of stanzaic patterns. He could compose a technically accomplished sonnet. Blank verse, however, was his choice. Although Pope was not a favorite, Willis did employ the English poet's heroic couplets. The entire body of his verse shows many variants of ten-liners, octets, and sestets. Occasionally, he employed the ballad stanza.

His verse, like that of many of his American contemporaries, might be classified under headings like "sacred," "sentimental," "amatory," and "occasional." The posthumous 1868 edition, if analyzed, reveals that eighty per cent of the poems could be so classified, yet the greater number of his early poems were completely serious. The adaptations of Biblical events, which gained wide recognition because of his comparative youth at the time of their composition, included "The Sacrifice of Abraham," "Absalom," "Hagar in the Wilderness," and "The Shumanite." A few of these appeared in the 1827 edition; others such as "The Leper" and "Saul" were published in the *American Monthly Magazine*.

The opening lines of "Absalom" provide an example of these Biblical adaptations:

> The waters slept. Night's silvery veil hung low
> On Jordan's bosom, and the eddies curl'd
> Their glassy rings beneath it, like the still,
> Unbroken beating of the sleeper's pulse.
> The reeds bent down the stream.[22]

Regarding these works, literary historians generally agree with James Russell Lowell's evaluation in "A Fable for Critics": Willis' pieces were compounded of "inspiration and water."[23] While Willis did adapt many stories into metrical form, he did not infuse the verses with any intuitive insights; nor did he inject life into characters whom he depicted. Later nineteenth- and twentieth-century readers would no doubt classify them as able paraphrases, no more. But they retained an appeal for the religious readers of his own time and of later generations. The serious tone is dominant in the other poems of the 1820's and 1830's. The moral tone marked the early verse writing, although his *vers de société* introduced a lighter note.

In a significant number of poems which deal with the beauties of external nature or with the personally sentimental, he also followed the romantic tradition. When he lyrically directed the attention of readers to the changes in seasons and chronicled his reflections in reaction to these natural changes, he reflected the main current of romanticism which included the work of James Thomson, William Cowper, Samuel Rogers, and Thomas Campbell. Willis was well acquainted with the poetry of these authors; it is not surprising, therefore, that he emulated their style. "The Spring is Here" recalls the work of the Whartons (and even of Wordsworth) in its praise of the idyllic life close to nature:

> We pass out from the city's feverish hum,
>   To find refreshment in the silent woods;
> And nature that is beautiful and dumb,
>   Like a cool sleep upon the pulses broods—
> Yet, even there a restless thought will steal,
>   To teach the indolent heart it still must feel.[24]

The tranquillity of home life in "Idleness" approximates the tone of much of William Cowper's poetry.

> My merry fire
> Sings cheerfully to itself; my musing cat
> Purrs as she wakes from her unquiet sleep,
> And looks into my face as if she felt
> Like me, the gentle influence of the rain.[25]

The tone and the subject of his poem written for the senior class at Yale in 1827 are very much like the tone and the substance of Gray's "Elegy." The recurrence of the theme of transitoriness of human endeavor is similar to Gray's evocation:

> And the proud man shall tread it, and the low
> The pathway to the grave may be the same
> With his bow'd head, shall bear him company.[26]

The more personalized expression of grief as in "On the Death of the Young Girl" and the sad tone of "The Soldier's Widow" ally his poems with the productions of the Graveyard School. The first poem stresses a feeling of personal loss:

> We cannot feel
> That she will no more come—that from her cheek
> The delicate flush has faded, and the light
> Dead in her soft dark eye . . . [27]

Among the later romantics, Wordsworth and Coleridge no doubt influenced Willis' choice of subjects and style. Professor Gay Wilson Allen in *American Prosody* recognizes Willis' ability by citing his mastery of Wordsworth's blank verse line. A poem such as "Refreshing Retrospections" is related to many of Wordsworth's verses which combine individual reflection with description of natural elements:

> The merry lark
> Springs from his plumy nest, breasting the clouds.
> And showers his thrilling music, even till
> His tiny form is lost within the light.[28]

He employed blank verse in many poems in which he developed Wordsworthian themes, personal in the emotions depicted and detailed in the scenes of nature described: poems like "Reverie at Glenmary":

> My heart tonight
> Runs over with its fulness of content;
> And as I look out on the fragrant stars
> And from the beauty of the night take in
> My priceless portion . . . [29]

or "Thought while Making the Grave of a New Born Child":

> Yet have I chosen for thy grave, my child
> A bank where I have lain in summer hours,
> And thought how little it would seem like
>   death
> To sleep amid such loveliness.[30]

There is emphasis in "Dawn" upon the therapeutic quality of external nature: "The air/Is like a breathing from a rare world."[31] In "Roaring Brook" he focuses upon the poetic qualities which he finds in nature:

> I deem it . . . true philosophy in him
> Whose path leads to the rude and busy world,
> To loiter with these wayside comforters.[32]

"Waking Dream in Sickness," written at Yale in 1827, combines Wordsworth's blank verse with an expression of attitude that is Coleridgean:

> The night creeps wearily. I lit my lamp
> To hide the brightness of that morning star
> That mocks me with a sleeplessness like mine—
> Cold and glitteringly apart and alone![33]

Often in poems which contain reflections about nature, a submission to nature in moments of dejection, or a questioning of oneself, a reader may find in his verse moods depicted by Coleridge in such poems as "Frost at Midnight," "Reflections on Having Left a Place of Retirement," or "To an Evening Star."

Sentimental poems were frequently composed to accompany an engraving in an annual or a periodical and were therefore categorized by the author as "occasional." At times, he was directly inspired by a painting.[34] "Better Moments," "Saturday Afternoon," and "Contemplations" were written with particular engravings in mind; all were sentimental in tone. Lines from the closing of "Saturday Afternoon" are typical:

> But the grave is dark, and the heart will fail
>   In treading its gloomy way;
> And it wiles my heart from its dreariness,
>   To see the young so gay.[35]

In such verses, the emotion is accentuated; but Willis used the emotional without portraying either the characters or the situations in such a way as to evoke the emotion. Highly personal, and sometimes more sincere, in tone are the poems "Birthday Verses," "To My Mother from the Apennines," and "Lines on Leaving Europe."[36] All were written with his mother in mind; in the first of the three, he wonders:

> How is she changed since *he* was there
>   Who sleeps upon her heart alway—
> Whose name upon her lips is worn—
>   For whom the night seems made to pray—[37]

"Thirty-five" is another occasional-sentimental piece, a "*mezzo-cammin*" lyric in which the author reflects upon his past.[38]

Life in New York City inspired Willis to write "occasional" lyrics, some of which were humorous and provided glimpses of his reactions to urban life. The most readable of his poems for later generations might well be the lyrical vignettes of city life: "To the Lady in the Chemisette . . .," "The White Chip Hat," and "To a Coquette."[39] "The White Chip Hat" has a light touch:

> Surprising! one woman can dish us
> So many rare sweets up together!
> Tournoure absolutely delicious—
>   Chip hat without flower or feather—
> Well-gloved and enchantingly boddices [*sic*],
>   Her waist like the cup of a lily—
> And an air, that, while daintily modest,
>   Repell'd both the saucy and silly—
>   Quite the thing![40]

Although none is a great poem, each has a sparkling quality that may save it from oblivion.

It should be recalled that versifiers of Willis' era who could write simply and sentimentally so that they could be readily understood by a large portion of the reading public were assured of success. As an editor, Willis had discovered the formula of simplicity and sentiment. Although he did condemn poetry written in an extreme sentimentalist vein, he did write verses which must be categorized as sentimental.

His use of obvious similes matched his selection of subjects in the English sentimental tradition. He often took romantic themes and reclothed them for his American readers. He was most original when he described a natural scene at which he was looking. When he relied upon literature for inspiration, the result was often a weak dilution. Lowell, realizing this weakness, satirized Willis for it.

Willis was a master of a variety of forms, an able metrist. As Kenneth B. Taft ably puts it, he did "genuflect before the gods of . . . propriety."[41] Accused of being frivolous, Willis at one time asserted that many of his poems were "from the under-current of . . . [his] frivolity and they run deep."[42] Literary historians, however, might mark him down as most successful a versifier when he indulged his humor and treated lightly those social manners which he treated so well in his prose writing.

II *Purveyor of Culture*

Willis' knowledge of literature, his experience as prose writer and versifier, and his knowledge as editor of literary periodicals qualified him as a collector of popular poetry. Additionally, he had reviewed newly published volumes of poetry.

George Pope Morris had compiled the *Atlantic Club Book*, his first anthology, while Willis was abroad. Willis had this model to follow when he made the decision to edit an anthology, but there were many other works with which he may have been acquainted. He was most certainly aware of Samuel Kettell's *Specimens of American Poetry*.[43] During his college days, he probably knew *Miscellaneous Poems Selected from the U.S. Literary Gazette*.[44] He had reviewed another anthology while he was editor of the *American Monthly Magazine*, George B. Cheever's *The American Commonplace Book of Poetry*.[45] For many years before 1844, Willis and Morris had edited poetry pages in the *Mirror*, so that they had the knowledge of anthologizing. In that year, the two editors began publication of numbers of the *Mirror Library*. Because of its success, the two men in the following year gathered most of the material in these numbers into *The Prose and Poetry of America*.

As a result of the large increase in the number of books published in the 1830's (through the use of new cylindrical

presses and development of new paper-making methods), many
readers found that they could complete the reading of an entire story in book form long before the end of the many weeks
it took to unfold the story chapter by chapter in the issues of
a periodical. Aware of this situation, editors sought to hold
subscribers by offering extras (or supplements) which included
an entire novel or book of poems in a single issue. The supplement was then issued with the periodical.[46] Willis and Morris
issued extras for this reason and thereby met the competition
of other periodicals, such as Park Benjamin's *New World* which
had begun the practice.

Six of the extras were, in fact, miscellanies; for in each, the
editors selected the productions of many British and American
authors (and an occasional Continental writer as well) which
dealt with a particular subject. The groupings reveal what the
two editors believed would be saleable to the contemporary periodical reading public: "The Album of Love," "Songs for the
Sabbath," "Gems of Scottish Songs," "Sands of Gold" (prose
selections including works of Washington Irving and Eugene
Scribe), "Sacred Rosary," and "The Harp with a Sabbath Tone."
The poems of Thomas Moore supplied the contents of five more
extras: "National Airs," "Love of the Angels," "Irish Melodies,"
"Lalla Rookh," and "Evenings in Greece." Single extras were
devoted to the works of Charles Dibdin, Thomas Hood, Letitia
E. Landon, Mrs. Hemans, and Barry Cornwall.

The editors offered their own work in a number of supplements. Willis' essays "Letters from Under a Bridge," "Pencillings
by the Way," and "Lecture on Fashion" appeared separately.
In two other extras, Willis' play *Tortesa* and "Sacred Poems"
were printed. And there were separate volumes devoted solely
to Morris' work.

Although prospectuses of the *New York Mirror* specifically
stated that special attention would always be given to native
productions, Willis and Morris, in selecting what they termed
"treasures of the few" for the delight and edification of their
readers, liberally drew upon the productions of English and
Continental writers. The reprints were mainly taken from
foreign magazines and newspapers. They reprinted poems by
contemporary English poets including Wordsworth, Coleridge,
Byron, Moore, Campbell, Hood, Southey, Landor, Elizabeth

Barrett, Tennyson, and Cornwall. Among prose writers, Dickens'
works appeared most often. Selections from Marryat, Martineau,
Mitford, Lamb, Hunt, Hazlitt, Thackeray, Mrs. Trollope, and
Charlotte Brontë also appeared in each of the journals.

Excerpts from the works of French and German writers also
appeared in the *Mirrors* and the *Home Journal*. Most popular
among the French writers were de Kock, Balzac, Scribe, De
Musset, and Sand. Poems by La Fontaine, Lamartine, Béranger,
Gautier, and Merimée were published. As for the German
writers, works of Schiller, Goethe, Richter, Tieck, Korner, and
Uhland appeared.

In reprinting the works of English, French, and German
authors, Willis and Morris contributed to widening the reputation of these writers in America. The editors consistently did
not hold with those American critics who recommended the
publishing of "native" productions alone. In addition to acquainting readers with international literary productions, they reported
foreign literary news. Reprinting such material made the editors
the purveyors of many European romantic literary conventions.

For Willis and Morris, the readers' knowledge of this poetry,
prose, and news was basic to their acquiring "cosmopolitanism"
and "culture," which the editors believed should be the hall-
marks of the citizens of the young republic.

III *Romantic Playwright*

During his editorship of the *American Monthly Magazine*,
various editorials and the "Scrap Book" revealed his interest in
the theater.[47] Among the authors whom he read, Willis regarded
Shakespeare as the master of all the Elizabethan and Jacobean
playwrights.[48] In the "Scrap Book" for November, 1829, Willis
pictured himself reading to Cousin Sybil from Ford's *Lovers'
Melancholy*. He then went on to write: "I love these old drama-
tists of Shakespeare's time—Ford and Webster and Heywood.
There is something about them—I do not know what—but it
quickens the blood strangely."[49] He consciously compared these
writings with those of his own day.[50] "The subjects of the old
writers," he noted, "were infinitely stronger, and deeper, and
more real than ours. We dare not paint an everyday human
passion." He liked the "bold relief" of their plays, the "true

colors." If the plays were to be produced in his time, he felt
that Shakespeare's language would be too direct for nineteenth-
century audiences.

On the American stage, "romance was in the air" in the early
1830's.[51] The influence of the English romantics was widely
felt. The Americans exploited Italy, according to Professor
Ralph P. Boas. American playwrights "found that their audiences
relished sensational love if it were non American."[52] The romantic dramatist, to be understood, naturally turned to the repre-
sentation of human emotional drives. Robert Montgomery Bird
did much to establish a trend in the romantic drama even as
Irving had for the sketch and the tale. Bird turned to historical
characters and scenes,[53] and James Lawson and Mrs. Elizabeth
Ellet in New York City turned to Italy for the setting of
their plays in their attempts to revivify history.

Willis followed in this romantic dramatic tradition when he
composed his two plays *Bianca Visconti* and *Tortesa the Usurer*.
It was natural for him to choose romantic subject matter since
he had in the 1820's and 1830's been attracted by the stories
of faraway places in his essays, travelogues, sketches, and poetry.
Such a metrical tale as "Lord Ivan and His Daughter" was con-
ceived in dramatic form, although the daughter speaks very
little in the poem. In his dramatic writing, he was to follow
his penchant for the romantic, the tragic, and the historical; and
he was to employ the blank verse form with which he was
most adept.

He continued a prize winner (for he had been such as a
versifier in the 1820's) in writing *Bianca Visconti;* it was written
in competition for an award by Miss Josephine Clifton for the
best play suited to her peculiar talent.[54] Willis chose the
person of Francesco Sforza as the character about which to
center the dramatic action of the play, and his repeated iden-
tifications with those of "natural nobility" fully explain the
choice. All the characters in the play are three-dimensional.

Willis chose to open the first act in a light, comic vein to
secure the interest of the viewers; the main action of the play
soon gets under way when a page reports that Sforza probably is not going to marry Bianca Visconti (to whom he has
been betrothed) because of the father's opposition to her wedding someone of low birth. Willis supplies sufficient villainy

throughout the play by his presentation of the character of Sarpellione, an Iago-Machiavelli figure, who early reveals that Bianca was born out of wedlock. He discloses the fact to make a stronger case against the planned marriage. Sarpellione states that the Visconti's son is alive and is the true heir to the Count's title and estate. In the play, viewers discover that this is none other than Giulio who has come with Sarpellione from the Naples and has disguised himself as the page in the court.

Among Sarpellione's other political plans is one to enlist Sforza's help for the Neapolitan king in conquering Florence. When this arch-plotter does not succeed, he plans to kill Sforza. He tries to get the court poet Pasquali to be the assassin thinking him a malcontent. Pasquali's rejection of the villain's request provides a sample of the type of verse Willis used throughout the play:

> When next you want a hand for your bad deed
> Look to your equals—there are those beneath you
> Who, from their darkiling wells, see guiding stars
> Far o'er your head, my lord.[55]

Despite opposition the marriage does take place; the viewer learns, however, when Sforza himself is on stage, that he fears Bianca does not really love him because he is not courtly enough and is too much the "rough and ready" soldier. As a result he withdraws from Bianca who becomes extremely melancholy, for she is in fact deeply in love with him. In a highly emotional soliloquy, she questions:

> He must love me,
> Or I shall break my heart! I never had
> One other hope in life! I never linked
> *One* thought, but to this chain. I have no blood
> No breath—no being—separate from Sforza.[56]

In subsequent scenes, Sarpellione manages to secure Brunario, one of Sforza's officers, to assassinate the hero. In a separate scene in the same act important to the plot's development, Sforza, in sword practice with the page, recognizes Giulio as the Visconti's son. Momentarily, he is tempted to kill him, but Giulio's graciousness changes his mind.

With the death of Bianca's father, the plot moves forward with her revelation to Sarpellione that she plans to give the crown to her husband. This information triggers the villain's plot to kill Sforza as he takes his daily rest. The plot is overheard by Bianca who in turn plans to have Giulio lie in the place where normally Sforza sleeps. Giulio, drugged by Bianca, is subsequently killed in error by Brunario.

In a lively last act, Pasquali captures Sarpellione and forces him to return to the court of Florence; Bianca becomes deranged after Giulio's death. After Sforza is crowned, Bianca regains her sanity long enough to speak the ironic and pathetic lines:

> Well, you loved me not
> And Giulio did—and somehow you should hate me
> If he were duke; and so I killed him, *loving me*
> For you that *loved me not.* Is it not strange
> That we can dream such things? The manner of it—
> To see it in a play would break your heart—[57]

Bianca dies after Sforza has felt contrition too late.

Tortesa the Usurer was written two years after *Bianca Visconti*; it too was derived from an Italian source. Shakespeare's plays provided models for elements of Willis' characterization and his setting. With the theme of love conquering all, it had, consequently, a wide romantic appeal for contemporary audiences.

In the play, Tortesa is betrothed to Count Falcone's daughter, Isabella.[58] Here as in the earlier play, the father opposes the planned marriage. The Count, however, agrees to the marriage in the hope that Tortesa will help restore his lands to him. Tortesa for his part is anxious for the social position which he will gain as a result of the marriage.

The play is complicated by the introduction of other actions: Falcone and the Duke of Florence confuse the identity of Angelo (a painter) and his old servant Tomaso. Impressed by his work, the Duke commissions Tomaso to do a portrait of Isabella. Angelo naturally takes Tomaso's place and paints Isabella; he falls in love with her and during one sitting is attacked by a jealous Tortesa.

In subsequent scenes Zippa, who is envious of Tortesa, seeks to prevent his marriage. At one point in the drama, the intricacy (and Willis has made it unduly complicated) of the plot leads readers to misinterpretations as to who loves whom; Isabella loves Angelo; Zippa confesses her love for Angelo to Isabella; and Isabella in disguise visits Angelo's studio to view her portrait, only to discover one of Zippa.

To avoid marrying Tortesa, Isabella drinks a potion which feigns her death. When she revives, she is refused entrance to her own home; for her father believes she is a spirit. Tomaso takes her to Angelo's studio which is raided by Tortesa and his men, since Angelo is believed to have stolen Isabella's corpse. When Tortesa parts the curtains where Isabella's portrait is supposed to be, he sees what he believes to be a picture; in actuality, it is Isabella standing immobile. In the denouement, Tortesa pleads for Angelo's pardon and praises the portrait of Isabella who, he feels, has been immortalized. He asserts his unworthiness for Isabella's hand; but when the truth of the situation is revealed to him, he duels with Angelo.

Before the final uniting of Angelo and Isabella and of Tortesa and Zippa, the audience is given a picture of Tortesa's basic nobility—underlined by Isabella's statement of his worthiness.

Despite the intricacy of the plot, the stage action never pauses. Willis, always aware of his audience, provided the right proportion of love, humor, and intrigue. The characters are individualized, and in the case of both Angelo and Tortesa they are ambivalent. The sympathy that the audience has probably felt for Angelo would inevitably shift for a brief while in the final act. The dialogue is generally successful, many of the metaphorical speeches being in a neo-Shakespearean vein. Willis used his experience with blank verse in *Tortesa* to good effect.

The merits of the play led Edgar Allan Poe, in his review of the drama, to state that it was "by far the best play from the pen of an American author." Poe recognized that it was good theater, although he felt that it suffered from many minor defects. Many actions, he pointed out, were inconsequential to the main plot—particularly those of Zippa. According to his standards, however, he found merit in its being natural and truthful "in sentiment and language."[59]

CHAPTER 7

Knickerbocker Spectator and
Home Journalist

I *Metropolitan Magazinist*

THE PERIOD between the publication of the *National Press*
and Willis' death roughly encompassed a score of years
which were the busiest of his career. His life centered about
the co-editorship of the *Home Journal*. During the 1850's and
1860's, Willis turned mainly to writing letter-essays and columns
for the *Journal*. Many essays were composed during or shortly
after the events described. Although they do not measure up
to the quality of the earlier *Pencillings*, many reveal that Willis
never lost his ability to write vivid description.

In 1846, after Willis and Morris had left the *Evening Mirror*
and *Weekly Mirror*, they attempted to edit a new weekly, the
National Press. After eight months, however, the newspaper
was renamed the *Home Journal*—a title, they felt, which better
signified their aims and interests. They had found that too
many people thought the *National Press* to be solely a political
organ. Their editorial responsibilities were divided very much
the way they had been before Hiram Fuller had become partner
in the earlier venture. Willis, who disliked the business details
of subscription, printing, circulation, and advertising, devoted
his energies mainly to writing articles attractive to readers.
Despite many periods of illness, Willis continued to compose
his weekly letters to Morris from Europe, Washington, the
West Indies, Idlewild, or from wherever he was traveling or
was recuperating.

The prospectus that the editors printed on November 21,

1846, is particularly interesting, for it shows distinctly the purposes they had in mind:

> To the circle around the family table we address the HOME JOURNAL. To the cares which intrude there, and which require to be softened and diverted and to the tastes and feelings which are there silently developing, and which need encouragement and culture, we seek to be a welcome visitor. Our aim will be to instruct, to refine, and to amuse. In a population as overworked as ours, there should be a ministration at home, of a different spirit from the excitements out of doors. Something to divert the mind should be ready to meet the tired man on his return from the day's toil. . . . In addition, however, to the entertaining features of the *JOURNAL*—its narrative, anecdote, humour, poetry and art—we shall give such a summary of news as will make the reader sure that he *loses nothing worth knowing of the world's goings on.* A periodical is wanted we think which picks, arranges, condenses, and gives in small compass, the "cream and substance" of the week's wilderness of newspaper reading, while, at the same time, the greater portion of its space is devoted to matter which is instructive, companionable, and amusing.[1]

Important, of course, was the editors' decision to report society news. It is also significant that this statement re-emphasized their aims to amuse, to refine, to instruct. The stress upon these goals allied the weekly with the earlier publications with which the two men had been connected. There were indeed overtones of earlier statements of the appeals to the family, the enumerations of literary features, and the stress upon taste and culture. But this 1846 prospectus was as clear a presentation of aims as the editors had ever made. The stress upon the convenience it provided the reader through its brevity, so that an article could be read quickly, anticipated numerous advertising appeals of twentieth-century magazines. The editors used new methods to interest prospective customers in the weekly. They offered their product to the "tired" businessman as something he could read to advantage in his leisure hours; they proffered it as an antidote to the practical concerns of the day.[2] There were significant omissions. Although news in brief form was to be included, political news was not.

Willis and Morris extended their editorial aims in later editions of the *Home Journal*. On January 1, 1848, they expressed the desire to have the journal "bubble over" with the news of Knickerbocker and European "gay life." Serious news was reduced to bare facts and outlines. In the social sphere, however, a "watchful eye" was kept "upon the agitations of this great metropolis." The editors' chronicling of news centered about a "searching for, a translating, a selecting of information" of fashions and fashionable gossip. They asserted that their paper was for the few, "the more refined individuals."[3] To assure the loyalty of women readers and subscribers, the editors addressed remarks to them pointing out that the periodical was produced for the intellectual and social élites.

The techniques to make the weekly "the Mirror of the fashionable world" were not new. They continued including translations of fashion news from the French newspapers and giving a prominent place to excerpts from London society journals. As active participants in New York social life, they reported upon events under a variety of column titles: "Uptown Correspondence," "Prittle Prattle," "The Season and Society," "Memos for Gossip," and "Chats in Town."[4] They were able to provide this extensive social reporting through the co-operation of ladies in society. These correspondents, "through their gifted and refined mediums," were kept apprised of all that occurred, "new, charming, or instructive in the brilliant circle of city life."[5] Often the editors were themselves guests at a gay soirée, such as Anne Lynch's famous Valentine Party in 1848 which Melville, Bayard Taylor, John Inman, Bryant, and Halleck attended.[6] In addition to the tidbits of gossip passed on to the editors by the anonymous female members of the social and literary coteries, chit-chat about foreign circles was forwarded to Willis from acquaintances in Europe. Columns dealing with such subjects as the *affaires de coeur* of the famous Lola Montez did not want for readers.[7]

Just as Willis had received criticism in Boston before 1831, so now did other journalists criticize the *Home Journal* for the space it devoted to subjects that these men considered "levity and folly." Willis breezily answered his critics that, since the millenium had not come, some had to do the office of providing the light touch. Unless he did it, "gayeties would then go undescribed, novelties unsketched, the bubble of the moment unseized, foreign eccentricities and humors untranslated, lovely women unportrayed."[8]

Female readers had a wide choice proffered them. Serial features on the lives of outstanding society women were included. Columns discussed questions of social propriety; articles were written on welfare, diet, posture, dress, and manners. But Willis and Morris did not forget their male readers. They felt that there were too few "highly cultivated and accomplished men" in town society. Articles published in the *Home Journal* which would instruct and refine, they hoped, would overcome this deficiency. Underlying their comments about refinement and taste was an avowedly serious purpose (according to one editorial statement): "The keeping open of a bridge of human sympathy and kindly feeling between the upper classes in the cities and the country at large." It was felt that there was much "literature" on the market which widened the chasm between these two classes. The *Home Journal* envisioned the development of a new group, an "aristocracy of the mind," who would act as the civilizers of American life.[9] They pictured "American Society" as a "rapidly fluctuating amalgam of the well born and the wealthy." The editors wanted to draw these two groups together with the intellectuals into an "expanding," "charming" circle.[10]

The *Home Journal* was quite outspoken about contemporary mores; but contemporary politics was another matter. This weekly was not political "at a time when politics filled the thought and dreams of Americans to an extent hard to realize today."[11] Turning away as it did from politics, the paper retained its popularity with Whig and Democrat, Northerner and Southerner. Even nine days after South Carolina dissolved its ties with the Union, the *Home Journal* reprinted, under the title "Kind Words from the South," a statement from the *Virginia Sentinel* that the *Journal* was one of the "best weeklies published in the Union. *It is entirely neutral in politics, free from all sectionalism and sectarianism.*"[12] Not until the Confederacy became a fact on June 15, 1861, did the editors express their own opinions. On that date, the periodical endorsed a public letter from Edward Everett to a Southern friend which stated that the action of establishing the Confederacy was an "act to bring on the war."[13] On May 28, 1861, Willis had been named a member of a committee—which included, among others, Peter Cooper, Horace Greeley, Bryant, and Charles Dana—charged with asking Everett to speak in New York for the Union cause. In May, it was decided that Willis would write "War Sketches" to present a "living chronicle of the war."[14] One week later, he began his "Lookings-On at the War." In their decision to report the war as completely as they were able, the editors were returning to a previous policy of close attention to national news.

The Civil War, however, turned the attention of many readers away from purely local matters to subjects of national concern. In the decade immediately preceding the war, many Knickerbockers had retired or were connected with moribund periodicals. The enthusiasm associated with these writers in the 1820's and 1830's was dissipated.

II *Periodical Littérateur*

The *Home Journal* editors in the 1850's continued their interest in the Knickerbocker tradition by printing the work of New Yorkers and by publishing many essays on the geography and the history of the metropolis. The editors' strong belief in the manifest destiny of New York as the "literary center of periodicals" was closely related to their continued devotion to Knickerbockerism.[15] For example, the *Home Journal* devoted as much space to the personality and works of Washington Irving as had any of its journalistic predecessors, reprinting his most popular sketches and essays, and publishing new prose pieces.[16] Willis, too, contributed a series of articles about Irving and Sunnyside.[17] In addition to a long and laudatory obituary on Irving in 1859, the editors printed other Irving items.[18] Among the other Knickerbocker writers, Paulding was not forgotten. Many of his sketches were reprinted. They also printed the work of other associates in the *Home Journal*: Theodore Fay from his diplomatic post in Europe contributed two sketches, and the work of Charles Fenno Hoffman and Gulian Verplanck was republished.[19]

Nor were the Knickerbocker poets neglected. Four of Woodworth's poems were revived, as well as verses by Drake, Wetmore, and Halleck.[20] William Cullen Bryant's poems were published for the first time. The *Home Journal* printed verses by poets who were not New Yorkers such as Longfellow, Holmes, Whittier, Read, and Sprague.[21] The South was represented by only two authors: Henry Timrod and Paul Hamilton Hayne. A separate column, however, was devoted to the poetry of the South as late as September 22, 1860.[22]

Willis paid attention especially to the poems of the new generation of authors of New York City. Bayard Taylor's ability, for example, had been first recognized by Willis when Taylor was an apprentice in the printing office of the *New Mirror*.[23] Later, the *Journal* printed the work of Taylor, but the poems of Thomas B. Aldrich were equally as popular. The other contributors—Richard H. Stoddard, William Winter, and Fitz-James O'Brien—were all associated with New York literary groups.[24]

The *Home Journal* continued to devote many columns to printing the work of the popular poetesses. This decade was, after all, the "feminine fifties." Female members of the New York literary groups were represented in the work of Frances S. Osgood, Anne C. Lynch, and Grace Greenwood.[25] Other contributions were made by Sarah T. Holton, Frances A. Fuller, Julia Ward Howe, and the Cary sisters, all favorites with contemporary audiences.[26] Also popular with readers were the works of the female story tellers and writers of sketches. Willis and Morris printed the contributions of "Fanny Forester," "Grace Greenwood," and Caroline M. Kirkland in the 1850's and 1860's.[27] Fanny Fern's work appeared for a short time in 1854 before Willis (her brother, for she was Sara P. Willis) ordered his editorial assistant Parton to accept no more work from her. Willis' decision seemed to be completely arbitrary since the subject matter and the tone of her work were similar to those of the other women whose work the *Journal* continued to publish.[28]

Following the previously established practices of the late *Mirrors*, the editors reprinted in the *Home Journal* supplements, essays, editorials, and original articles with short "reviews" of published works. Invariably, critical notices had no more detailed analysis of style or of content than the notices in the earlier journals. Successful as were many of the features of the weekly, they did not improve the critical notices nor bring them up to the standards that they themselves had announced in editorial columns. A critical notice was generally, as before, composed of two parts: the reviewers' brief impressionistic comment followed by a pertinent excerpt to illustrate points touched on in the introductory statement. Books, dramatic and musical productions, and lectures were treated in similar fashion. The notices did, however, keep readers informed of current publications and hopefully whetted appetites.[29]

Although none of the critical remarks was distinctive, a few may be mentioned as representative. Whittier, always a favorite with Willis, was praised for his "earnestness and his nationality."[30] The reviewer, probably Willis, observed that Whittier outdid all his contemporaries in his "fierce sincerity." Longfellow's wide popularity was discussed in observations about his *Poems of the Seaside and Fireside*.[31] There was none before him in the "sympathies of the book buyers."[32]

If column space is any measurement of recognition, substantive attention was given to the work of Herman Melville. Evidence indicates that Willis was fairly well acquainted with Melville, whom he had probably met a few times at Anne Lynch's parties. Moreover, there is no doubt that the two authors had been in contact with each other in the 1840's and 1850's. The *Home Journal* favorably reviewed *Mardi, Redburn,* and *White Jacket. Mardi* was welcomed as "one of the most agreeable events of the season," an observation based solely on personal sympathy for the author. This same review looked forward to a confident future for Melville: a "good many seasons" would see a "good book from a man of genius." These words are indeed ironic in view of Melville's fading reputation during the years that remained in the century. Intuitive or impressionistic as Willis' words may be, the twentieth-century discovery of the author of *Mardi* has at least justified the use of the word "genius." No attempt was made to explain the allegory in *Mardi* or its satire, although Willis' literary background provided him with the basis for understanding.[33] The review asserted pride in the British praise of Melville—a point which would identify the article as Willis', for he knew firsthand the British publishers and British reading public. The article ended by calling the work "exquisite."

"Simplicity of style" and "truthfulness of manner" were the two elements of Melville's *Redburn* mentioned in another review. *White Jacket* was praised for the same characteristics, but the reviewer observed that there was "little or nothing of connected dramatic narrative" in the work. The "fresh and abundant" humor of the book was, however, recognized.[34] As with Poe, so with Melville: Willis sensed the works of geniuses without completely understanding the nature of the authors.

When Hawthorne's *Blithedale Romance* was reviewed in the *Home Journal,* the article commented upon the author's stylistic abilities and particularly upon his power of portrayal of characters.[35] Favorable comment was given Thoreau's *Walden* in 1854. The adjectives "unique" and "graphic" were applied to the work. The writer, again probably Willis, recognized "its original vein of reasoning and its earnest introspection."[36]

The *Home Journal* was as faithful in its reporting of the drama as the old *Mirrors* had been, for the editors commented upon productions each week. Events involving any stage or opera star were given extended treatment. Both editors had had their plays produced in New York. Both men were close friends of actors and producers. Full reporting was given to such events as the Pierce Butler divorce of actress Fanny Kemble, a popular figure of the day. The MacReady Riots at the theater on Astor Place were reported in detail.[37] Willis wrote a special essay on Jenny Lind, and separate reviews were devoted to each of her appearances. When the actor Edwin Forrest attacked Willis because of the editor's defense of Mrs. Forrest, the *Home Journal's* column required no special novelties by the author to assure sales for that week's issue. Mrs. Forrest had for some time been a close friend of Willis and his wife. As a consequence of these events, Willis was later involved in litigation proceedings following the Forrest divorce case.[38]

Other artists also knew that they had sympathetic friends in the editors of the *Home Journal.* Art exhibitions held in the city were visited and then described for the edification of readers. Certainly, this action was consistent with the editors' desire to carry "culture" to the readers. A letter from the artist William Mount to Morris may have led to an editorial by Willis on the "Business Position of Artists."[39] The plea it expressed paralleled statements in defense of writers and public support of literary people. It castigated the Art Union for its unfair treatment of artists and expressed the hope that in the future the artists would be "treated as an honorably productive class, not as objects of charity."[40] The weekly at different times published articles on Mount and on two friends of Willis: Washington Allston and Horatio Greenough.[41] Willis had known both men from his Boston days. His extensive travels in Europe and his experience with art and artists made him fully qualified as an art reviewer.

The editors' concern with the plight of the artists was related to their continuous crusade for proper recognition of, and adequate pay for, authors and editors. This attitude also reflected their concern with those whom they identified as members of the "aristocracy of the mind."

The *Home Journal* succeeded primarily because of the editors' relationship. The two men, devoted magazinists, expended all their energies in its publication. Indefatigable as both men were, they were entirely opposite in personal temperament: the personality of one man complemented the other. Morris brought to the partnership an able business sense and an extensive knowledge of printing. His conscientiousness and congeniality made him a valuable partner who dealt directly with the public, publishers, and other editors. Willis, urbane, literary, and witty, brought to the partnership his extensive talents in writing in a wide variety of fields especially suited for the periodical— sketches of manners and morals, travel essays and letters, short stories, and poems. It was he who brought the "smart set naughtiness" to the *Journal* with just the right amount of worldliness to stir readers and titillate the gossips. When the editorial aims of the *Journal* are considered in terms of amusement and instruction, it must be concluded that Morris' cautious editorial counseling tempered Willis' wit with a middle-class morality, even as Willis enlivened the morality of the weekly with wit. The unity and homogeneity of tone characteristic of the weekly through its years of publication until the time of the Civil War was, therefore, the result of the two men and of a small staff of magazinists who assisted them. Both men happily had an excellent talent of choosing literate, able, and conscientious young men as aides.

Although the *Home Journal* had readers in many parts of the Union, it did not attempt to satisfy the tastes of a national audience; nor, on the other hand, did it become so specialized in one type of subject matter that variety was lost. In summary, the weekly addressed itself primarily to a New York reading public by continuing to combine sophistication and sentimentality on its pages. For home readers, the editors succeeded in effecting a union of domesticity and culture. Tales, sketches, poems, and essays about elements of home life were included for those "around the family circle."

Social and fashionable news, which had been of secondary importance in the earlier publications, became one of the primary concerns of the editors. In addition to making the magazine an arbiter of fashion, Willis and Morris wanted the *Journal* to be an instrument of culture and refinement. To achieve this end, the editors offered what they considered the best articles and columns on fashionable modes of dress and deportment, as well as the best literary productions of the day. They repeatedly emphasized their function of careful selection—picking, condensing, and arranging their material for their "select" body of readers.

CHAPTER 8

Chronicler and Critic of the Times

I *Travel Sketcher*

WILLIS acquired his initial reputation as a versifier in the 1820's, and he gained in the same decade extensive editorial experience which accounted for his ultimate success as a professional magazinist. In the 1820's he also began the writing of travel sketches, many of which were employed in the composition of his fictional narratives culminating in *Paul Fane.* Abroad in Europe in the 1830's, he strengthened his contemporary reputation by writing lively travel sketches for the *New York Mirror.* These were edited later as *Pencillings by the Way.* Interspersed with the many reprints of his tales, sketches, and poems are volumes of miscellaneous material in which are included travel essays, reflective essays, portraits of outstanding contemporaries, editorials, and periodical items on a variety of subjects. Such works include *Rural Letters . . ., Letters from Under a Bridge, Hurrygraphs, Health Trip to the Tropics, Famous Persons and Places, Outdoors at Idlewild,* and *The Convalescent.* Their publication gives further evidence of Willis' many talents and versatility. Willis' was indeed a wide canvas when we consider the scope and variety of the works.

In the vein of *Pencillings* are many successful essays about his travel in the United States, Europe, and the Near East. Willis printed in his *Inklings* a rewritten letter, containing material that had been used in an earlier letter which had been lost in transmittal. It was about the time when he had just completed his tour in the Near East. Labeled by the author as "A Log in the Archipelago," it centered about his trip from the Near East in 1832. Willis depicted scenes from his voyage aboard the American brig *Metamora* from Smyrna to Malta. Either waiting for sailing or on board ship, Willis had adequate time for reflecting and "musing on the mundane and proximate matters."[1] He thought of various mythological and historical associations as the ship passed ancient places. The details of a furious passage were narrated excitingly, as was the final scene before he was put ashore at Malta. There was some hesitation on the part of the captain about altering his course, and for a while Willis thought he was to be carried all the way back to the States. He appealed to the captain's kindness as a fellow countryman and with much relief began his hegira north.[2]

From Willis' varied experiences in the 1830's came the travel essays grouped under the title of "Sketches of Travel," which were early published in *Loiterings*. Nearly all are about his trips to various parts of the British Isles. Here were gathered his reactions to the streets of London, the crowds on the London Strand, the traffic jams of Bond Street, and the details of society equipages. Memorable were his short chapters devoted to Stratford, Warwick Castle, and Kenilworth. The sketch of his arrival is representative, and the tone and overtones are Irvingesque:

> I chose my room from among the endless vacant but equally luxurious chambers of the rambling old house; my preference solely directed by the portrait of a nun, one of the family in ages gone by—a picture full of melancholy beauty, which hung opposite the window. The face was distinguished by all that in England marks the gentlewoman of ancient and pure descent; and while it was a woman with the more tender qualities of her sex breathing through her features, it was still a lofty and sainted was the work of a master, probably Vandyke, and a picture in sister, true to her cross, and sincere in her vows and seclusion. It which the most solitary man might find company and communion.[3]

As he did repeatedly in his sketches in *Pencillings*, he successfully evoked the spirit of the place by imagining the landscape in the past. Willis visited Shottery and imagined looking at it with Shakespeare's eyes. He wrote: "How daringly the imagination plucks back the past in such places."[4] He pondered over Will's relations with Anne: "Did she know how this common and often terrestrial passion becomes fused in the poet's bosom with celestial fire, and, in its wondrous elevation and purity, ascends lambently and musically to the very stars?"[5] When he arrived in Stratford, Willis thought of the way in which people regarded Shakespeare: "It is painful and embarrassing to go to Stratford—to reconcile the immortality and the incomprehensible power of genius like Shakespeare's with the space, tenement, and circumstance of a man."[6]

In his essay on Kenilworth, he balanced his comments by expressing his disenchantment with and his appreciation of the place:

> Kenilworth, as it now stands, would probably disenchant almost any one of the gorgeous dreams conjured up by Scott's romance. [The visitor] . . . sees a fretted and ivy-colored ruin, relieved like a cloud castle in the sky; the bright blue plane of the western heavens shining through the window and broken wall, flecked with waving and luxuriant leaves and the crusted and ornamental pinnacles of tottering masonry and sculpture just leaning to their fall though the foundations on which they were laid, one would still think, might sustain the firmament.[7]

Part of *Loiterings of Travel* was devoted to essays presenting scenes of Washington at the end of a Congressional Session. There is nothing outstanding among these reports except the obvious effort by Willis to dispel any misconceptions the British reading public may have had about the capital. Looking at the boys climbing on railings waiting to catch a glimpse of President-elect Van Buren led Willis to suggest that the scene would have been a fit subject for the painter Veronese.[8] In mock-heroic tone, he described the quiet in Washington after the session had ended.[9] Basically, his evaluation is one of praise for Washington: "Within a half hour's gallop, you have a sylvan retreat of every variety of beauty, and in almost any direction. . . . You have all the seclusion of a rural town, and none of its petty politics and scandal—all the means and appliance of a large metropolis and of its exactions and limitations. That which makes the charm of a city, and that for which we seek the country, are equally here, and the penalties of both are removed."[10]

"Passages from an Epistolary Journal," written in 1839, did not measure in quality to that of his earlier travelogues. He was not so successful in description, nor did he succeed completely in bringing to the reader his enthusiasm and prejudices. In them, he made observations about a visit to Bedlam, a Brighton coach, a dinner for MacReady, and the magnificence of London shops. He was taken aback by the London railroad station and particularly by its "Brobdignag roof."[11]

Willis was able in 1840, after contracting with the British publisher George Virtue, to write short chapters for W. H. Bartlett's book of sketches, *American Scenery*. He realized a hope that he had earlier expressed when he edited the *Legendary*, for he assembled "as much as possible of that part of the American story which history has not yet found leisure to put into form, and which romance and poetry have not yet appropriated —the legendary traditions and anecdotes. . . ."[12] The range of views was comprehensive and gave ample opportunity to indulge his favorite avocation—the chance of looking over material which he enjoyed. The natural sights which were favorites with European visitors and American excursionists were Niagara Falls, the Palisades, the Hudson River, the Highlands, the Susquehanna, and Virginia's Natural Bridge. Balancing these views and written sketches were pictures and commentaries of cities and towns: Yale University, the Erie Canal, Morris' home at Undercliff, Bunker Hill, Mt. Vernon, and the White House. Willis' comment about the city is representative: "Distance lends more enchantment to a view of Washington than to most other views." Willis was impressed by Washington winter society with its "company of highly cultivated and superior men."[13]

In *Rural Letters*, actually not published until 1856, Willis reprinted many letters which he had sent to the *National Press* from fashionable American watering places such as Sharon Springs or from his home at Glenmary. Most of them are written in his usual chatty style and are adequately done. There are flashes of wit and piquancy in a few passages such as the one in which he aims a barb at Boston, or in which he describes the primping of a young lady: "And, even in the faces of the Bostonians of whom there are several families at Sharon the indefinable holier-than-thou-ativeness which is the phylactery of common wear in that exemplary city—relaxes here."[14] Or he writes of a young lady in Trenton Falls: "One of the girls (a tall figure, like a woman in two syllables connected by a hyphen at the waist,) continued to look at the back of her dress in the glass, a la Venus Callipage."[15]

Willis' *Hurrygraphs* and his *Health Trip to the Tropics* are additional collections of travel essays. Those of the former volume, printed in 1850, included letters which Willis sent to the *Home Journal* from various points in New England. *Hurrygraphs*, as the name implies, also included portraits of popular personages. In the travelogues, Willis sketched, as was his custom, with something of a painter's eye. For example, the people living on Cape Cod appear to him as fine studies for painters.[16] He described the places in his "framework" by focusing on carefully delineated details. Not only did his eye carefully watch for such scenes, but he consciously attempted to "catch the speech"—"the unmitigated Cape pronunciation."[17]

In the same work, he revealed that he had been on a scenery hunt into the regions newly opened for travelers by the Erie Road. While he appreciated the speed of the railroads in making beautiful spots available, he also imagined himself as a traveler "whirling past" and sometimes getting as a result an "erroneous impression" of a place. He included letters about Lake Mahopac, Greenwood Lake, Ramapo, and Westchester. He foresaw many of these locations as suburbs of New York; the railroads would soon, he felt, "irrigate the country with refinements, in contrast with which these primitive sketches may be curious."[18]

The 1853 *Health Trip to the Tropics* included letters written during 1852 from Bermuda and various Caribbean islands such as St. Thomas, St. Pierre, Martinique, and Haiti. Also reprinted were letters from Mammoth Cave, Kentucky, and New Orleans. Again his attention was upon the characteristics that differentiated a place and upon unusual people. In Martinique in April, 1852, he wrote of the Negro inhabitants and particularly of Mlle. Juliette Celestine, whose house he had visited. He included in his letter a brief discussion of intermarriage and of segregation in St. Pierre. He was delighted by the "*tableaux vivants*" in the streets, the holiday costumes, and the general festive air In comparison with New York, he felt that St. Pierre was much pleasanter since there were no pig sties or shanties "out of town."[19]

Other letters about Mammoth Cave were adequate reports of

the place, but failed to give the fine examples of imaginative, impressionistic description of which he was capable. He fell into the habit of quoting extensively from other works, a practice he had earlier deplored. In Kentucky, among other places, he visited a village of Shakers. In Lexington, he observed what he termed "negro comfort well distributed instead of white wretchedness filthy in a heap."[20] Harrodsburg had scenes that he would have had Darby sketch for the "rudeness and the grotesqueness of real life groupings."[21]

He wrote too of Haiti's "Eden of a climate."[22] Havana's cathedral was "like a gorgeous design by Turner's . . . pencil."[23] Southern cities in the United States made deep impressions on Willis. Savannah he enjoyed as a "Vallambrosa of retreat."[24] Charleston was a "town built for gentlemen."[25] Further on, he mused on the effect of railroads erasing distance whereas stage coaches "used to punctuate, emphasize, and make it intelligible."[26]

Willis composed a delightful recipe to indicate the composition of New Orleans:

"3/4 purposes and pleasures of fashionable society"
"1/3 sidewalk uses of Broadway"
"moderate portion of Wall Street, stirred till it effervesces"
"a pinch of gossip and Fine Arts, hilarity at discretion, and a
    sprig or two of such 'going-it-strong.' "[27]

Sounding notes that he later repeated many times in the *Home Journal*, that he had in fact stated in the earlier journals, Willis gave a "Lecture on Fashion" in 1844. The thoughts which went into this work were the result of seventeen years of travel and association with the members of "society" in many countries and in various parts of the United States. Quite realistically, he saw that "the vicious, the wilful, the ignorant, and short sighted" were in the majority in America's large cities.[28] It was against this condition that he hoped for the establishment of an aristocracy of the intellect. "Fashion" he defined as a "position in society attained by different avenues in different countries." He appeared to suggest the "sphere of fashion" of Paris as a model.

Although he had been successful as a journalist in Great Britain, Willis indicated in this lecture that there were humiliations awaiting any literary lion in England. Again he brought up the question of which he had treated in his short stories, that of "nature's stamp of superiority."[29] The latter qualification was certainly no "passport to fashion in New York." In America, he perceived that extravagance too often took "the place of intellect or nobility of nature."[30] He anticipated Veblen at least in one phrase regarding what he considered the perversion of fashion—he termed it "conspicuousness in expense."

He expressed regret about the large proportion of "evil" in the population; and he called public opinion "unexamined, unauthorized, uncontrolled."[31] He hoped frankly for a change, for he noted that America did have "intellect"; it did have "nature's nobility"—"men of spirit and bearing, and women of such talent and beauty, as would draw homage alike from the Indian on the Prairie, or the exclusives at Almack's."[32]

Hurrygraphs included, in addition to travel sketches, reprints of editorials on fashion. In "Fashion and Intellect in New York," Willis hopefully pointed out that New York had the material for as brilliant a society as any place in the world. Realistically, however, he felt that the "Aristocracies of Brain and Pocket [would] ... not come together in the natural course of things during" his generation.[33] In similar essays on society in America, he once again indicated that there was an "aristocracy of God's endowing." In America, he felt the need for a code of etiquette because of the lack of politeness and the general devotion to the "national principle" of "getting on."[34] Besides this quality, Americans he felt were highly mobile; there was also an "uncertainty of men's fortunes and positions."[35] Related to these subjects was an essay which constituted Willis' rationale for his society reporting, "The Propriety of Sketches of Fashionable Society." The leaders of fashion, Willis felt, "should be responsible to public criticism." Also, they forfeited their privacy because of their position. He, as a reporter, would "... equalize the prize of public admiration to all customers."[36]

His gallery of portraits included Emerson, Fields, Cooper, Poe, and Morris. The perceptive sketch of Emerson was representative: "his voice is up to his reputation. ... in delivery, his cadences tell you that the meaning is given ... when—flash!—comes a single word or phrase, like lightning after listened out thunder, and illuminates, with astonishing vividness, the cloud you have striven to see into."[37]

Four other works which may be grouped together are "Letters from Under a Bridge," *Outdoors at Idlewild, Rural Letters,* and *The Convalescent.* All have many personal essays comprised of reflections on the places where Willis lived. They reveal his deep-seated feelings about the locations to which he liked to retire. One such place was the "brook hollow of Glenmary": "It spread wide as it drops upon the meadow, but above like a book that deserves its fair margent, it deepens as you proceed."[38] In essays which anticipate Thoreau by a few years, Willis is a close observer of nature who feels "it fun to lie still and watch all the animal life that stirs when they think the human being has gone."[39] His favorite haunt was under a bridge where it was both cool and calm. Although a lover of the metropolitan and gay life, Willis wrote: "I have always fancied there was a mixture of the vegetable in myself; and I am convinced now, that there is something in us which grows more thriftily on fresh earth, than on flagstones."[40] Addressing many of these letters to his doctor, he wrote: "I have fallen into a sad trick, dear Doctor, of preaching sermons to myself, from these texts of nature."[41]

Actually, Willis was "recovering" at Glenmary, he said, from what he called the "hotel fever"—acquired in his traveling. He repeatedly marveled at the newness of much that he saw as he roamed over his property. He sensed the beauty of the "intangibles on a piece of property" that was to be sold. Letter III was a stock-taking of what he considered important. Earlier in life, he felt that he had had many false values—placing emphasis upon "knowledge and the parade of knowledge." For Willis, the "perfection of existence" seemed to be "to possess the arts of social life, with the simplicity and freedom of savages."[42]

Something of the peace and recuperative spirit which Willis had gained in Pennsylvania at his Glenmary home was similar to what he experienced at Idlewild, the name given to his New York country home on the banks of Canterbury Creek near the Hudson River. In 1852, he purchased a tract at Cornwall, and on it he built a large gabled cottage. From his home, he sent a series of letters which were later brought together by Scribner's for publication in book form. Many of them in tone and style resembled the earlier "Letters from Under a Bridge."

A few of the letters written in 1853 and 1854 have relevance for twentieth-century readers because of the predictions which he made. The age of speed, he felt, would make the Hudson an "extension of Broadway."[43] His letters of early 1854 referred to Newburgh as being "at the end of a long street of New York."[44] In similar fashion, he felt that Idewild was "on Chambers Street," for the traffic on the river was so very heavy. The area seemed to him ideal for those who have "rural tastes and metropolitan refinements rationally blended." He wanted to leave as much of his "seventy acre world" as natural as possible, "seeing how far a place can be improved by originating nothing." "You get," he wrote, "such large effects with so little labor...." He confessed: "We dread being reminded of what is going to do [*sic*] just as well *without us*."[45]

One letter is memorable because of its description of West Point. Willis singled out the commandant for praise, "being certainly in feature, mien, and manner, the perfection of what they [the cadets] should study for a soldier."[46] At the time of writing, Willis had no idea that he was praising the future general of the Confederacy—Robert E. Lee.

Finally, *The Convalescent* followed the pattern of *Outdoors at Idlewild*, for it purported to be no more than letters about new events. Willis did not even attempt to make them into essays since, as he said, he wanted to retain the flavor of the originals. His thoughts again circle around the seasonal changes at Idlewild, or around the life there.

Perhaps the most important, as well as the most memorable letters reprinted in this edition, are the letters originally written for the *Home Journal* in July and August of 1857 about an interview with Washington Irving. As Willis approached the time of the meeting, the old question arose in his mind about what might be considered an intrusion of privacy. On this score, Willis had been criticized for his English letters: "It is a question somewhat mooted, just now, you know, how far may be thus used if at all, the privileges of hearth, friendship, and relationship."[47] After reading Irving's own "Abbotsford," he felt that the question was answered for him and that he was justified in making the visit. Willis pictured Irving at his writing desk and closely transcribed the nature of the conversations he had with him. He considered traveling through Sunnyside with Irving as analogous to traveling through "Fairyland with Spenser."[48] "The playful and affectionate reciprocity between Geoffrey Crayon and his readers, is the key-note of Washington Irving's life at home."[49]

Another passage suggested his reaction to the setting: "A more beautiful intricacy of hill and dale than that winding road through Sleepy Hollow, I never saw. Everything in it seemed so precisely of the enjoyable size—woods, meadows, slopes, thickets and cornfields, all in the come-at-able and cozy quantity that looks just what you want too little for care."[50] And, in trying to analyze Irving's charm, Willis wrote: "I have brought away the impression, however, I may venture to say, that a *modesty* amounting almost to diffidence (a narrow escape, perhaps, of a want of sufficient self-confidence for the world we live in), and a most unusual degree of *instinctive deferential courtesy*, are the two natural qualities at the bottom of it."[51] The letters indeed bring full circle Willis' admiration for Irving, for the younger writer had early emulated "Geoffrey Crayon." Willis always held Irving in the highest respect; the *Home Journal* letters give evidence of the deep feeling he had for the Knickerbocker writer.

In Willis' *Prose Works* a long section was entitled *Ephemera*. Here he gathered miscellaneous items gleaned from the columns of the various journals for which he worked. Most of these short passages were properly identified by the title, for they were topical and transitory. Here and there among them, however, were examples of graphic reporting from close observation on the scene. Such was the report of the slum area near Five Points in New York City. The scene was something out of Dickens. Willis' reaction after a detailed, almost naturalistic, description recalls Melville's Redburn's reaction to the poverty of Liverpool: "For one, I had never before any adequate idea of poverty in cities. I did not dream that human beings within reach of human aid, could be abandoned to the wretchedness which I there saw—and I have not described the half of it. . . ."[52]

Or Willis has the ability, as well as a saving sense of perspective, to picture lionizing in London, a process to which he himself was subjected: "The fact is, that the position of a mere literary man in England, in any circle above that to which he is born, is that of a jackal. He is invited to the entertainment of the aristocratic lions and lionesses who feed him. He has neither power nor privilege in their sphere."[53]

One passage addressed to readers showed the keenness with which he was able to judge his audience's wants. It epitomized, too, the feeling that many readers had about periodicals—they wanted the curt, the trivial, the quickly read. So, he asked a rhetorical question: "What shall it be? If we understand you rightly, you would prefer on this last page, some well contrived nonsense—to wind off trippingly, as it were. Wisdom is respectable. Pictures, poetry, prose, pathos, and puffery are all very well—but after being instructed, you wish to be let out of school. Is that it?"[54]

CHAPTER 9

"The Profession of Taste"

I *Magazinist par Excellence*

A CLOSE EXAMINATION of Nathaniel P. Willis' work shows that his achievements were appreciable in many fields. Facts point to the conclusion that he was a conscientious, hardworking journalist and editor. In Poe's words, he proved himself a magazinist par excellence. In collaboration with Morris, Willis showed himself an alert innovator inaugurating many departments which reflected readers' special interests. He not only had a shrewd sense of public taste, but he constantly exercised remarkable perception in recognizing new or latent talent.

Willis, not the oversensitive person he has been sometimes pictured as being, had a saving sense of humor, was able to turn the joke upon himself, and was often aware of the ephemeral quality of much of his work. As a writer, he was intensely devoted to his craft. He was seriously concerned with the recognition of literature as a profession. As an editor he was able to give voice to the problems which concerned many American writers, such as the matter of an international copyright treaty.

Successful in the tradition of Irving in writing the familiar essays, he achieved fame as one of America's earliest foreign, social correspondents and as a reporter of travels. In the travel essays, his talents shone the strongest; his prose was clear, sharp, and nimble. He conveyed well his enthusiasm for viewing new places, and the freshness of his observations sustained the lively quality of the essays. Never forgetting that periodical readers expected to be amused, Willis wrote letters and essays from many points on the Continent and in England which were witty and entertaining in treatment of society life. Professor Wegelin has praised the chattiness of Willis' travel letters and the range of subject matter.[1] Professor Daughrity feels that a reading of his prose is "indispensable,"[2] if one wishes to study the development of interest in the field of international manners. In fact, the essays about the *haut monde* had the widest appeal among middle-class American readers.

Among other non-fictional works, Willis' essays, composed in what seemed a reflective mood about the beauties of natural scenes, are not without merit. He showed himself a close observer of nature and a master of detail in picturing his impressions. Additionally, he was able to portray in selective descriptive phrases outstanding contemporaries. Short critical essays and reviews of various authors show too that he was extremely perceptive in recognizing the qualities of genius in particular writers. Later generations of critics have confirmed his remarks about such writers as Poe, Melville, Whittier, Emerson, and Cooper. Many times he characterized accurately the foremost abilities of Washington Irving.

In fiction, Willis contributed distinctly to the short story with his surprise ending, a technique used extensively later by O. Henry. He was very often as successful in building suspense as Poe was in his Gothic tales. His structure appears best in stories which have a single narrator about which the events of the story center. When he relied upon his personal experiences, he proved he could transmute actuality into believable fiction. When he adapted plots from others, he was not as successful.

Willis should also be credited with continuing the treatment of society and social manners to which Cooper had paid attention in many novels. His effort in the novel *Paul Fane* earns for the author the title of a forerunner of James in the examination of the international theme. Whereas much of his fiction may be read with interest today, his poems are less successful. His verses which still retain degrees of liveliness are vignettes about New York life.

The importance of his anthologies lies in their comprehensiveness and in their acquainting a wide number of readers with American and European belles-lettres. To the literary and cultural historians, the anthologies indicate the relative popularity of certain authors during decades of the nineteenth century.

Although Willis' two plays *Bianca Visconti* and *Tortesa the Usurer* may be termed period pieces, they do show that he had a good ear for dramatic dialogue, a sense for the right dramatic scene, and the ability to write flexible blank verse.

Finally, his achievement in magazine journalism may be measured by the extent that the periodicals for which he had responsibility brought American writers and readers into fruitful relationship. These periodicals aided American authors by providing a medium of expression and also by supplying models for further literary work. In other words, since literature creates literature, the emulation by native talent of forms, ideas, and styles (such as were to be found in the *Home Journal*) contributed to the establishment of new, as well as the strengthening of old, literary vogues.

II *"Profession of Taste"*

Through Willis' efforts the *Home Journal* became a self-appointed instrument of refinement and an arbiter of fashion. Willis, ever alert in answering readers' needs and wishes, provided week after week vicarious enjoyment for those who emulated members of New York society—a sizeable segment of the periodical-buying group of the middle-class reading public. He was a journalistic pioneer in combining features on domesticity and culture to produce a non-political magazine-newspaper for the housewife, the businessman, and the littérateur. The *Home Journal* used the writing talents of many able young writers and aided them in establishing themselves as magazinists—men whose profession was the preparation of periodicals.

With the advantage of one hundred years' hindsight, one can see that Willis' last periodical especially pointed toward the "quality" magazines of the twentieth century which stressed the cultivated, the elegant, and the genteel. In the expanding literary spirit, evident in America in the ante-bellum decades, however, a significant number of literary tendencies reached a wide public; and literary talent secured an outlet through the periodicals he co-edited.

Willis, then, attempted to deliver his readers from the commonplace which Irving had once said pervaded much of American life. He deplored the situation in America where extravagance and expense too often took the place of intellect or nobility of nature. He felt that "men of science, distinguished artists, poets, and authors" were not sought out for their intellectual accomplishments. Basically, Willis in his serious editorial writing upon society, confronted in his time the questions which are again being posed by such men as John Gardner in the twentieth century regarding the demands of excellence versus those of equality.

His work is representative of many aspects of pre-Civil War literature; he made appreciable contributions to literature and to journalism. In the latter field, he successfully established a sophisticated, cosmopolitan tone in periodical literature, a quality emulated by many later editors. As Professor Quinn has suggested, students should not neglect in their American studies, the urbanity and the generosity of this man with a zest for the good life.[3] If past literary historians have stressed only the ephemerality of many of his productions, this present work has attempted to strike a balance by highlighting his accomplishments. Willis' continual striving to raise the literary profession, his own pride in his chosen field, and his expressed hopes for the expanding of cultural achievement and good taste among people, as well as his wish for the recognition of intellectual accomplishment—all these deserve attention and possibly reconsideration just as much as his perception deserves praise.

Notes and References

Preface

1. Edward F. Haywood, "Nathaniel Parker Willis," *Atlantic Monthly*, LIV (1884), 216.
2. Kenneth L. Daughrity, "The Life and Work of Nathaniel Parker Willis, 1806-1836" (unpublished doctoral dissertation, University of Virginia, 1935), p. v.
3. Edgar Allan Poe, "Nathaniel P. Willis," in *The Complete Works of Edgar Allan Poe*, ed. James A. Harrison (New York, 1902), VIII, 325.
4. Oliver Wendell Holmes, "Introduction" to *A Mortal Antipathy* (Boston, 1892), p. 4.
5. Arthur Hobson Quinn, *The Literature of the American People* (New York, 1951), p. 222.

Chapter One

1. Daughrity, p. 9.
2. *Ibid.*, p. 22.
3. *Ibid.*, p. 23.
4. Henry Beers, *Nathaniel Parker Willis* (Boston, 1885), p. 48.
5. Poe, p. 322.
6. *The Legendary* (Boston, 1828), I, v.
7. *Ibid.*, II, 96.
8. "Preface," *The Token* (Boston, 1829), pp. i-ii.
9. *Ibid.*, I, 150. Reprinted in the *New York Mirror*, VI, 125.
10. *American Monthly Magazine*, I (April, 1829), iii.
11. *Ibid.*
12. Frank L. Mott, *A History of American Magazines* (Cambridge, 1939), I, 577.
13. *American Monthly Magazine*, I (April, 1829), iii.
14. *Ibid.*
15. *Ibid.*, p. iv.
16. Poe, p. 325.
17. *American Monthly Magazine*, I (August, 1829), 355.
18. *Ibid.*, p. 356
19. *Ibid.*, p. 357.
20. Poe, p. 322.
21. See *passim American Monthly Magazine*, I (November, 1829), 549; II (July, 1830), 270-71; II (October, 1830), 477.

22. *Ibid.*, I (September, 1829), 438.
23. *Ibid.*, I (October, 1829), 494.
24. *Ibid.*, I (November, 1829), 579.
25. *Ibid.*
26. *Ibid.*, I (December, 1829), 619.
27. *Ibid.*, p. 647.
28. *Ibid.*, I (March, 1830), 866.
29. Poe, p. 324.
30. *American Monthly Magazine*, I (January, 1830), 731-32.
31. *Ibid.*, II (February, 1831), 780.
32. Fred Lewis Pattee, *The Development of the American Short Story* (New York, 1923), p. 78.
33. Note especially the following, all in the *American Monthly Magazine:* I (July, 1829), 274; I (August, 1829), 357; I (September, 1829), 379 and 428-30; I (October, 1829), 486, 495, and 507; I (December, 1829), 646, 653; I (January, 1830), 688, 700; II (March, 1830), 12; II (April, 1830), 69; II (May, 1830), 134; II (June, 1830), 193, 208, 160-66; II (July, 1830), 270, 282-83; II (August, 1830), 350, 354, 364; II (September, 1830), 417; II (January, 1831), 692; II (February, 1831), 726; II (March, 1831), 841; III (June, 1831), 211; III (July, 1831), 272-73.
34. *Ibid., passim.*
35. *Ibid.*
36. See the *American Monthly Magazine*, III (May, 1831), 113 ff.; I (December, 1829), 589; II (January, 1831), 690; I (September, 1829), 379 ff.; I (November, 1829), 532 ff.
37. *Ibid.*, II (June, 1830), 161.
38. *Ibid.*
39. *Ibid.*, III (July, 1831), 272-73.
40. See the *American Monthly Magazine*, I (April, 1829), 54-63; I (June, 1829), 203-13; II (June, 1830), 172 ff.; II (August, 1830), 368 ff.
41. *Ibid.*, II (April, 1830), 18-25; I (June, 1829), 195-200; III (April, 1831), 39-44; II (March, 1831), 835-39.
42. *Ibid.*, I (June, 1829), 200-3; III (June, 1831), 149-55; I (September, 1830), 365-67; II (February, 1831), 725; II (December, 1830), 581-85.
43. *Ibid.*, I (August, 1829), 354.
44. *Ibid.*
45. *Ibid.*, I (April, 1829), 33.
46. *Ibid.*
47. *Ibid.*, II (February, 1831), 726.
48. *Ibid.*, I (May, 1829), 108.
49. *Ibid.*, p. 109.

50. *Ibid.*
51. *Ibid.*
52. *Ibid.*
53. *Ibid.*, II (January, 1831), 692.
54. *Ibid.*, I (August, 1829), 323.
55. *Ibid.*, I (March, 1830), 867.
56. *Ibid.*, II (April, 1830), 68.
57. *Ibid.*, III (April, 1831), 56.
58. *Ibid.*
59. Beers, pp. 89-99.
60. *New York Mirror,* III (March 9, 1826), 255.
61. *Ibid.*, IX (September 10, 1831), Editorial.
62. *Ibid.*, IX (September 24, 1831), 95.
63. *Ibid.*
64. *Ibid.*, IX (April 14, 1832), 327.

Chapter Two

1. *Pencillings by the Way* (New York, 1844), Letter I, p. 1. (Hereafter referred to as *Pencillings* with letter number and page number.)
2. *Pencillings,* III, p. 4.
3. *American Monthly Magazine,* I (July, 1829), 241-45.
4. *Ibid.*, p. 243.
5. *Ibid.*
6. *Ibid.*
7. *Pencillings,* p. xii.
8. *Ibid.*
9. *Ibid.*, I, p. 2.
10. *Ibid.*, IV, p. 6.
11. Beers, p. 113.
12. *Pencillings,* XXI, p. 35.
13. *Ibid.*, XIV, p. 21.
14. *Ibid.*, X, p. 15.
15. *Ibid.*, XIV, p. 22.
16. *Ibid.*, XII, 19-20; V, p. 7; IX, p. 15.
17. *Ibid.*, XIX, p. 31.
18. *Ibid.*
19. *Ibid.*, V, p. 8.
20. *Ibid.*, XXI, p. 33.
21. *Ibid.*
22. *Ibid.*, V, p. 7.
23. *Ibid.*, IX, p. 14.

24. *Ibid.*, XXVII, p. 44.
25. *Ibid.*, XXIX, p. 47.
26. *Ibid.*, XXX, p. 47.
27. *Ibid.*, XLV, p. 65.
28. *Ibid.*, XXX, p. 48.
29. *Ibid.*, LXXIX, p. 121.
30. *Ibid.*, LXXXIII, pp. 127, 129.
31. *Ibid.*
32. *Ibid.*, LXXXVI, p. 132.
33. *Ibid.*, XC, p. 140.
34. *Ibid.*, CV, p. 165.
35. *Ibid.*, LXXXIV, p. 130.
36. *Ibid.*
37. *Ibid.*, CIX, p. 172.
38. *Ibid.*
39. Robert Spiller, *The American in England* (New York, 1926), p. 364.
40. *Pencillings*, CXV, p. 180.
41. *Ibid.*, CXVI, pp. 182-83.
42. *Ibid.*, CXVII, p. 185.
43. *Ibid.*, CXXII, p. 193.
44. *Ibid.*, CXVIII, p. 186.
45. *Ibid.*, CXXIX, p. 202.
46. *Ibid.*
47. *Ibid.*, X, p. 15.
48. *Ibid.*
49. Kenneth L. Daughrity, "Poe's 'Quiz on Willis,'" *American Literature*, V (November, 1933), 55-62.
50. Beers, pp. 154-55.
51. *Ibid.*, p. 161.
52. *Ibid.*, pp. 72-78.
53. *Ibid.*
54. *New York Mirror*, XI (August 17, 1833), 52.
55. *Ibid.*, XI (September 7, 1833), 76.
56. Roy Allen Billington, *The Protestant Crusade, 1800-1860* (New York, 1938), p. 53.
57. *New York Mirror*, XI (November 16, 1833), 159.
58. *The Letters of Willis G. and Lewis G. Clark*, ed. L. W. Dunlap (New York, 1940), p. 89.
59. *New York Mirror*, XII (April 18 and 25, 1835), 332, 340.
60. *Morning Courier and New York Enquirer*, VII (April 29, 1835), 2; *National Intelligencer*, XXIII (May 6, 1835), 2.
61. *New York Evening Post* (May 7, 1835), 2.
62. *New York Mirror*, XVI (October 20, 1838), 133.

63. *Ibid.*, XVI (November 10, 1838), 159.

64. Dunlap, *Letters*, p. 112.

65. See the statement which appeared in the *Corsair*, I (March 16, 1839), 16.

66. *New Yorker*, VII (May 25, 1839), 157.

67. *Corsair*, I (June 1, 1839), 185.

68. *New York Mirror*, XX (July 30, 1842), 247.

69. Gordon N. Ray, *Thackeray: The Uses of Adversity, 1811-1846* (New York, 1955), p. 200.

70. Harold H. Scudder, "Thackeray and N. P. Willis," *PMLA*, LVII (June, 1942), 589-92.

71. Ray, p. 271.

72. Scudder, pp. 590-91.

73. *Ibid.*, p. 596; Beers, p. 256.

74. William M. Thackeray, *The Adventures of Philip* (New York, 1899), p. 520.

75. *New Yorker*, IX (April 18, 1840), 15.

76. *Corsair*, I (March 16, 1834), 16.

77. The original manuscript, in the Yale University Library, is dated June 23, 1836.

Chapter Three

1. Men like Benjamin Day of the *New York Sun* and James Gordon Bennett of the *New York Herald* were pioneers in selling cheap newspapers. Horace Greeley was among the first New York journalists to realize the appeal of this type of daily.

2. *New Mirror*, II (October 7, 1843), 2.

3. *Ibid.*, III (April 20, 1844), 48.

4. *Ibid.*, III (August 3, 1844), 286.

5. *Ibid.*, III (May 25, 1844), 127-28, and III (September 28, 1844), 416.

6. Gay Wilson Allen, *The Solitary Singer* (New York, 1955), p. 65. He cites Walt Whitman, *Unpublished Prose and Poetry*, ed. Emory Holloway (New York, 1932), I, 161, f.n.

7. George E. Woodberry, *The Life of Edgar Allan Poe* (Boston, 1909), II, 101.

8. Letter to Joseph Field of June 15, 1846, in John W. Ostrom (ed.), *The Letters of Edgar Allan Poe* (Cambridge, 1948), II, 318.

9. *New York Mirror*, VIII (May 7, 1831), 349.

10. *Ibid.*, XVII (December 20, 1839), 215.

11. Clarence S. Brigham, "Edgar Allan Poe's Contribution to *Alexander's Weekly Messenger*," in *Proceedings, American Antiquarian Society*, LII (April 5, 1942), 61.

12. *Ibid.*

13. Woodberry, II, 85.

14. Quoted by T. Cottrell Clark, "The Late N. P. Willis and Literary Men Forty Years Ago," *Northern Monthly*, II (November, 1867-April, 1868), 236.

15. *Home Journal*, IV (October 20, 1849), 2.

16. Pointed out in a letter to the author from Professor T. O. Mabbott, a recognized Poe scholar.

17. "Authors' Pay in America," *Evening Mirror*, I (October 10, 1844), 2; "The Pay for Periodical Writing," *Evening Mirror*, I (October 12, 1844), 2.

18. Woodberry, II, 115.

19. *Evening Mirror*, I (January 29, 1845), 4.

20. *Ibid.*, I (January 14, 1845), 3; I (January 17, 1845), 3; I (January 21, 1845), 1, 2.

21. *Home Journal*, IV (October 20, 1849), 2. Willis took great care to stress Poe's punctuality when he worked for the *Mirror*.

22. *Weekly Mirror*, I (November 30, 1844), 122.

23. *New Mirror*, III (April 6, 1844), 16.

24. *Ibid.*, I (June 24, 1843), 192.

25. *Ibid.*, II (April 5, 1845), 2.

26. *Ibid.*, I (November 20, 1844), 2.

27. *Ibid.*, I (February 5, 1845), 2.

28. See *Weekly Mirror*, II (April 19, 1845), 24; *Evening Mirror* I (January 30, 1845), 2; II (May 2, 1845), 2; II (May 16, 1845), 2.

29. See *Evening Mirror*, I (January 3, 1845), 2.

30. *Ibid.*, I (December 21, 1844), 2.

31. *New Mirror*, I (May 20, 1843), 109.

32. *Weekly Mirror*, II (July 26, 1845), 245.

33. *Evening Mirror*, I (December 21, 1844), 2.

34. *Ibid.*, I (March 10, 1845), 2.

35. *Ibid.*

36. *Ibid.*, II (April 24, 1845), 2.

37. *Ibid.*, II (May 31, 1845), 2.

38. *Ibid.*, II (September 29, 1845), 2.

39. *Ibid.*, I (October 7, 1844), 2.

40. *Ibid.*

41. *New Mirror*, III (June 8, 1844), 159; III (June 29, 1844), 208.

42. *Ibid.*, III (June 15, 1844), 176.

43. *Evening Mirror*, I (October 12, 1844), 2.

44. *Weekly Mirror*, III (October 11, 1845), 32.

45. *Evening Mirror*, III (October 23, 1845), 1.

46. *New Mirror*, I (May 27, 1843), 128.

47. See *Evening Mirror*, I (January 2, 1845), 4; I (April 1, 1845),

4; III (November 18, 1845); II (August 21, 1845), 4; III (April 20, 1844), 36.

48. *New Mirror*, II (February 17, 1844), 320. Cited by Albert H. Smyth, *Bayard Taylor* (New York, 1946), p. 62.

49. *Ibid.*, III (June 8, 1844), 159; III (June 29, 1844), 208.

Chapter Four

1. Quinn, p. 214.
2. Washington Irving, "The Schoolmaster" from *Bracebridge Hall* in H. Pochmann (ed.), *Washington Irving* (New York, 1934), pp. 193-97.
3. *American Monthly Magazine*, I (November, 1829), 560.
4. *Ibid.*, I (March, 1830), 866.
5. Nathaniel P. Willis, *Inklings of Adventure* (London, 1836), I, v.
6. "Preface" to *Dashes at Life* in *Prose Works* (New York, 1845), p. 250.
7. *Ibid.*
8. "Preface" to *People I Have Met* (New York, 1850), p. vi.
9. *Ibid.*, p. viii.
10. Pattee, p. 84.
11. Kenneth B. Taft, *Minor Knickerbockers* (New York, 1947), p. lxxix. The review was from the *New York Review and Atheneum Magazine* of December, 1825.
12. "Preface" to *Rural Letters* (New York, 1849), p. vl.
13. *Ibid.*
14. The *Legendary*, II (1828), 96-107.
15. *American Monthly Magazine*, I (April, 1829), 54-63; I (June, 1829), 203-13.
16. The *Token*, I (1829), 150.
17. *Ibid.*, p. 151.
18. *Inklings of Adventure*, I, v.
19. *American Monthly Magazine*, III (July, 1831), 223, 224, 221-25.
20. *Ibid.*
21. *Ibid.*, p. 225.
22. *Ibid.*, II (April, 1830), 41-45; II (June, 1830), 172-79.
23. *Ibid.*, I (August, 1829), 313-21.
24. *Ibid.*, III (May, 1831), 77-81.
25. *Ibid.*, pp. 80-81.
26. *Ibid.*, II (October, 1830), 468.
27. *Ibid.*, I (August, 1829), 347-52.

28. *Ibid.,* I (June, 1829), 196.
29. *Ibid.,* II (April, 1830), 18-25.
30. *Ibid.,* II (May, 1830), 104.
31. *Ibid.,* (May, 1829), 93-107.
32. *Ibid.,* p. 94.
33. *Ibid.,* II (March, 1831), 835-39.
34. *Ibid.,* II (July, 1830), 290-92.
35. *Ibid.,* III (June, 1831), 192-96.
36. *Ibid.,* III (April, 1831), 39-44; III (May, 1831), 96-101.
37. *Ibid.,* II (May, 1830), 119-25.
38. *Ibid.,* p. 119.
39. *Prose Works,* pp. 361-66.
40. *Ibid.,* p. 405.
41. *Ibid.,* p. 404.
42. *Ibid.,* p. 406.
43. *Ibid.,* p. 410.
44. *Ibid.,* pp. 389-95.
45. *Ibid.,* p. 399.
46. *Ibid.,* p. 403.
47. *Ibid.,* p. 379.
48. *Ibid.,* pp. 366-69.
49. *Ibid.,* pp. 369-71.
50. *American Monthly Magazine,* I (November, 1829), 8.
51. *Prose Works,* p. 462.
52. *Ibid.,* pp. 379-83.
53. *Ibid.,* pp. 410-12.
54. *Ibid.,* pp. 429-33.
55. Among those items which comprised hack work was a description of Undercliff which appeared in *American Scenery* (London, 1842). See Beers, p. 247.
56. *Prose Works,* pp. 501-4.
57. *Ibid.,* pp. 504-6.
58. *Ibid.,* pp. 479-86; see *Pencillings,* CVII, p. 169.
59. *Ibid.,* pp. 348-52.
60. *Ibid.,* pp. 457-60.
61. *Ibid.,* pp. 479-86.
62. *Ibid.,* p. 484.
63. *Ibid.,* p. 486.
64. *Ibid.*
65. *Ibid.,* pp. 486-89.
66. *Ibid.,* pp. 445-54.
67. *Ibid.,* pp. 474-79.
68. Beers, p. 277.
69. *Prose Works,* pp. 281-83.

70. *Ibid.*, pp. 283-85.
71. *Ibid.*, pp. 489-501.
72. *Ibid.*, pp. 313-15.
73. *Ibid.*, pp. 300-6.
74. *Ibid.*, pp. 454-57; 264-72.
75. *Ibid.*, pp. 310-13.
76. *Ibid.*, pp. 528-30.
77. *Ibid.*, pp. 512-15.
78. William P. Fenn, "The Source of One of Willis' Sketches," *American Literature,* VI (January, 1935), 421-26.

Chapter Five

1. *Prose Works,* pp. 342-44.
2. *Ibid.*, p. 343.
3. *People I Have Met* (New York, 1852), pp. 256-73.
4. *Prose Works,* pp. 316-18.
5. *Ibid.*, pp. 466-74.
6. *Ibid.*, p. 466.
7. *Ibid.*, p. 471.
8. *Ibid.*, pp. 298-300.
9. *Ibid.*, pp. 278-80.
10. *Ibid.*, p. 280.
11. *Ibid.*, pp. 251-68; p. 268.
12. *Fun Jottings* (Auburn, 1855), pp. 276-95.
13. *Prose Works,* pp. 518-20.
14. *Ibid.*, pp. 335-36.
15. *Ibid.*, pp. 507-9.
16. *Ibid.*, pp. 318-23.
17. *Ibid.*, pp. 330-32.
18. *Ibid.*, pp. 352-56.
19. *Ibid.*, p. 336.
20. *Ibid.*, p. 337.
21. *Ibid.*, p. 338.
22. *Ibid.*, pp. 366-71.
23. *Ibid.*, pp. 372-77.
24. *Ibid.*, pp. 285-94.
25. *Ibid.*, pp. 289-90.
26. *Ibid.*, p. 294.
27. *Ibid.*, p. 345.
28. *Ibid.*, pp. 323-27.
29. *Ibid.*, p. 339.
30. *Ibid.*, pp. 341-42.
31. *Ibid.*, pp. 516-18.

32. *Ibid.*, pp. 272-74.
33. *Ibid.*, pp. 275-78.
34. *Ibid.*, pp. 326-30.
35. *Ibid.*, pp. 294-97.
36. *Paul Fane* (New York, 1857), p. 17.
37. *Ibid.*, p. 19.
38. *Ibid.*, p. 20.
39. *Ibid.*, p. 29.
40. *Ibid.*, p. 95.
41. *Ibid.*, p. 106.
42. *Ibid.*, p. 156.
43. *Ibid.*, pp. 206-18.
44. *Ibid.*, pp. 207, 280
45. *Ibid.*, p. 388.
46. *Ibid.*, p. 396.
47. *Ibid.*, p. 399.
48. *Ibid.*, p. 18.
49. *Ibid.*, p. 19.
50. *Ibid.*, p. 89.
51. Christof Wegelin, *The Image of Europe in Henry James* (Dallas, 1958), p. 14.
52. Christof Wegelin, "The Rise of the International Novel," *PMLA,* LXXVII (June, 1962), 305-10.

Chapter Six

1. Beers, pp. 48-49.
2. "Preface" to *Sacred Poems* (Mirror Library, 1844), p. i.
3. *American Monthly Magazine,* II (July, 1830), 285.
4. *Ibid.*, I (September, 1829), 420.
5. *Ibid.*, I (October, 1829), 486.
6. *Ibid.*, I (December, 1829), 594.
7. *Rural Letters* (Auburn, 1849), p. 190.
8. *American Monthly Magazine,* I (April, 1829), 33.
9. *Ibid.*
10. *Ibid.*, II (July, 1830), 258-59.
11. *Ibid.*, p. 258.
12. William Ellery Leonard, *Byron and Byronism in America* (Boston, 1905), p. 56.
13. *The Poems, Sacred, Passionate, and Humorous* (New York, 1868), p. 161. (Hereafter referred to as *Poems.*)
14. Leonard, p. 56.
15. *Poems,* pp. 195-96, 202-6, 216-17, 218, 247.
16. *Ibid.*, p. 205.

17. *Ibid.*, p. 206.
18. *Ibid.*, p. 313.
19. *Ibid.*, p. 319.
20. *Ibid.*, p. 315.
21. *Ibid.*, p. 347.
22. *Ibid.*, p. 44.
23. James Russell Lowell, "A Fable for Critics," in *The Poetical Works* (Cambridge, 1904), pp. 43-45.
24. *Poems*, p. 274.
25. *Ibid.*, p. 268.
26. *Ibid.*, pp. 230-31.
27. *Ibid.*, p. 252.
28. *American Monthly Magazine*, II (March, 1831), 834.
29. *Poems*, p. 119.
30. *Ibid.*, p. 91.
31. *Ibid.*, p. 229.
32. *Ibid.*, p. 276.
33. *Ibid.*, p. 199.
34. *Ibid.*, pp. 223, 121, and 108.
35. *Ibid.*, p. 121.
36. *Ibid.*, pp. 35, 98, 99.
37. *Ibid.*, pp. 95-96.
38. *Ibid.*, pp. 274-75.
39. *Ibid.*, pp. 281, 284-85, 305.
40. *Ibid.*, pp. 284-85.
41. Taft, p. xciv.
42. "Preface" to *Sacred Poems*, p. 6.
43. Boston, 1829.
44. Boston, 1826.
45. In 1838, Cheever edited a similar collection of prose.
46. Helmutt Lehman-Haupt, *The Book in America* (New York, 1951), p. 130.
47. See *American Monthly Magazine*, I (July, 1829), 264; I (January, 1830), 687.
48. *Ibid.*, I (July, 1829), 264.
49. *Ibid.*, I (November, 1829), 550.
50. *Ibid.*, I (January, 1830), 688.
51. Arthur H. Quinn, *A History of the American Drama from the Beginning to the Civil War* (New York, 1943), p. 220.
52. "The Romantic Lady," in *Romanticism in America*, ed. George Boas (New York, 1961), p. 69.
53. Quinn, p. 248.
54. *Ibid.*, p. 255.
55. *Ibid.*, p. 214.

56. *Ibid.*, p. 217.

57. *Ibid.*, p. 229.

58. *Tortesa the Usurer* in *Representative American Plays*, ed. Arthur H. Quinn (New York, 1953), pp. 249 ff.

59. Quoted by Quinn in *Edgar Allan Poe* (New York, 1941), pp. 283-84.

Chapter Seven

1. *Home Journal*, I (November 21, 1846), 2.

2. *Ibid.*

3. *Ibid.*, III (January 1, 1848), 2.

4. *Ibid.*, III (July 8, 1848), 2; VII (November 1, 1851), 2.

5. *Ibid.*, XII (November 22, 1856), 2.

6. *Ibid.*, III (February 19, 1848), 2.

7. *Ibid,* III (March 4, 1848), 2.

8. *Ibid.*, IV (January 20, 1849), 2.

9. *Ibid.*, XI (July 7, 1855), 2.

10. *Hurrygraphs* (New York, 1851), p. 168.

11. Basil Rauch, "The First Hundred Years," *Town and Country*, C (December, 1946), 64.

12. *Home Journal*, XVI (December 29, 1860), 2.

13. *Ibid.*, XVII (June 15, 1861), 3.

14. *Ibid.*, XVII (June 1, 1861), 3.

15. *Ibid.*, III (February 12, 1848), 2 and IV (July 21, 1849), 2.

16. See February and March, 1855, issues *passim*.

17. *Home Journal*, XIII (August 8, 1857), 1; XIII (August 15, 1857), 2; XIII (August 22, 1857), 2.

18. The obituary appeared in *Home Journal*, XV (December 10, 1859), 2; see also XV (December 24, 1859), 4; XV (May 28, 1859), 4; XV (December 31, 1859), 2; and XVI (May 5, 1860), 2.

19. *Ibid.*, XV (October 29, 1859), 1; III (November 11, 1848), 4.

20. Woodworth—*Home Journal*, III (June 10, 1848) or XVI (March 30, 1861), 4; Halleck—XI (March 10, 1855), 1; Wetmore—VII (April 13, 1851), 1; Drake—XII (June 7, 1856), 2; Bryant—III (September 30, 1848), 1.

21. Longfellow—*Home Journal*, IV (May 5, 1849), 1 and IV (December 22, 1849), 2; Holmes—IV (July 7, 1849), 4; Whittier—XI (February 10, 1855), 2; Read—III (February 5, 1848), 4; Sprague—IX (June 4, 1853), 1.

22. Timrod—*Home Journal*, XIV (August 29, 1857), 4; and Hayne—XI (July 14, 1855), 1. The special column appeared in XVI (September 22, 1860), 3.

23. *Ibid.*, XII (September 26, 1857), 1. This is only one entry of many.

24. Many issues carried Aldrich's work between XII (July 26, 1856), 2, and XV (February 19, 1859), 1; Fitz-James O'Brien—XII (October 18, 1856), 1.

25. Osgood—*Home Journal*, III (January 1, 1848), 1; Lynch—V (January 19, 1850), 1; Greenwood—X (December 23, 1854), 1.

26. Bolton—*Home Journal*, XVII (January 26, 1861), 2; Howe—III (December 23, 1848), 2; Fuller—IV (July 14, 1849), 4; Phoebe Cary—IV (November 17, 1849), 1.

27. Fanny Fern—*Home Journal*, X (January 21, 1854), 1; Grace Greenwood—III (January 22, 1848), 1; Kirkland—VI (November 16, 1850), 1.

28. His sister composed and published a novel, *Ruth Hall*, in which she satirized his personality and his action in this situation.

29. Hardly any space was set aside by the editors for discussions of literature or fiction. On October 7, 1848, the subject of "The Uses of Fiction" was briefly examined. The moral influence of the novel was praised. When a responsible novelist attempted to exert such an influence, he was to be regarded (the editors stated) as one of "Nature's ministers." This doctrine shows no departure from the criterion by which the editors examined earlier works of the *Mirrors*.

30. *Home Journal*, III (December 23, 1848), 3.

31. *Ibid.*, V (January 1, 1850), 2.

32. *Ibid.*

33. *Ibid.*, IV (April 21, 1849), 4.

34. *Ibid.*, IV (April 13, 1850), 1; IV (November 24, 1849), 2.

35. *Ibid.*, IX (July 31, 1853), 2.

36. *Ibid.*, X (October 7, 1854), 3.

37. *Ibid.*, IV (May 12, 1849), 2.

38. *Ibid.*, V (June 29, 1850), 2.

39. *Ibid.*, IV (November 10, 1849), 1.

40. *Ibid.*, IV (November 10, 1849), 1.

41. *Ibid.*, VII (December 20, 1851), 1 and VIII (January 17, 1852), 1; XI (November 3, 1853), 1; IX (August 13, 1853), 1.

Chapter Eight

1. *Inklings of Adventure*, III, 110 *passim;* see also *Prose Works*, p. 440.

2. *Prose Works*, p. 444.

3. *Ibid.*, p. 562.

4. *Ibid.*, p. 563.

5. *Ibid.*
6. *Ibid.*
7. *Ibid.*, p. 566.
8. *Loiterings of Travel* (London, 1840), III, 133.
9. *Ibid.*, p. 163.
10. *Ibid.*, pp. 165-66.
11. *Prose Works*, p. 535.
12. *American Scenery* (London, 1840), I, iv.
13. *Ibid.*, II, 50.
14. *Rural Letters*, p. 330.
15. *Ibid.*, p. 343.
16. *Hurrygraphs*, p. 47.
17. *Ibid.*, pp. 47 ff.
18. *Ibid.*, p. 109.
19. *Health Trip to the Tropics*, pp. 130-34.
20. *Ibid.*, p. 240.
21. *Ibid.*, p. 254.
22. *Ibid.*, p. 275.
23. *Ibid.*, p. 281.
24. *Ibid.*, p. 326.
25. *Ibid.*, p. 327.
26. *Ibid.*, p. 335.
27. *Ibid.*, p. 340.
28. "Lecture on Fashion," in *Complete Works* (New York, 1846), p. 801.
29. *Ibid.*, p. 803.
30. *Ibid.*, p. 807.
31. *Ibid.*, p. 809.
32. *Ibid.*, p. 810.
33. *Hurrygraphs*, p. 263.
34. *Ibid.*, p. 297.
35. *Ibid.*, p. 298.
36. *Ibid.*, p. 316.
37. *Ibid.*, p. 172.
38. *Prose Works*, Letter I, p. 217.
39. *Ibid.*
40. *Ibid.*, p. 218.
41. *Prose Works*, Letter IV, p. 224.
42. *Rural Letters*, p. 39.
43. *Outdoors at Idlewild*, p. 17.
44. *Ibid.*, p. 282.
45. *Ibid.*, p. 53.
46. *Ibid.*, p. 422.
47. *The Convalescent* (New York, 1859), p. 119.

48. *Ibid.*, p. 133.
49. *Ibid.*, p. 134.
50. *Ibid.*, p. 140.
51. *Ibid.*, p. 143.
52. "Ephemera" in *Prose Works*, p. 582.
53. *Ibid.*, p. 612.
54. *Ibid.*, p. 593.

Chapter Nine

1. Wegelin, *The Image of Europe,* p. 14.
2. Daughrity, p. 472.
3. A. H. Quinn, *History of the American Drama,* I, 255.

Selected Bibliography

PRIMARY SOURCES

1. Collected Works
The Complete Works of N. P. Willis. New York: J. S. Redfield, 1846.
The Prose Works of N. P. Willis. Philadelphia: Cary and Hart, 1849.

2. Anthologies
The Prose and Poetry of Europe and America. New York: 1857. (With George P. Morris.)

3. Books (Prose)
Inklings of Adventure. 3 vols. London: Saunders and Otley, 1836.
The Tent Pitch'd. New York: Colman, 1839.
American Scenery. 2 vols. London: Virtue, 1840.
Loiterings of Travel. London: Longmans *et al.*, 1840.
Lectures on Fashion. New York, Mirror Library, 1844.
Pencillings by the Way. New York, Mirror Library, 1844.
Rural Letters. Auburn: Alden and Beardsley, 1849.
People I Have Met. New York: Baker and Scribner, 1850.
Life Here and There. New York: Baker and Scribner, 1850.
Hurrygraphs. New York: Scribner, 1851.
Fun Jottings. Auburn: Alden and Beardsley, 1853. Reprinted 1855.
Health Trip to the Tropics. New York: Scribner, 1854.
Famous Persons and Places. Auburn: Alden and Beardsley, 1854.
Outdoors at Idlewild. New York: Scribner, 1855.
Paul Fane. New York: Scribner, 1857.
The Convalescent. New York: Scribner, 1859.

4. Plays
"Bianca Visconti," in *American Plays*, ed. ALLEN G. HALLINE. New York: American Book Co., 1935.
"Tortesa the Usurer," in *Representative American Plays*, ed. ARTHUR H. QUINN. New York: Appleton-Century-Crofts, 1953.

5. Poetry
Melanie and Other Poems. New York: Saunders and Otley, 1837.
Poems of Passion. New York, Mirror Library, 1844.
The Poems, Sacred, Passionate, and Humorous. New York: Clark and Maynard, 1868.

6. Newspapers, Annuals, and Journals
American Monthly Magazine, 1829-1831.
The *Corsair,* 1839-1840 (edited with W. O. Porter).

The *Evening Mirror,* 1844-1846 (edited with George P. Morris).

The *Home Journal,* 1846-1864 (edited with George P. Morris; initially called *National Press*).

The *Legendary.* Boston: Goodrich, 1828.

The *New Mirror,* 1843-1844 (edited with George P. Morris).

The *New York Mirror,* 1831-1839 (edited with George P. Morris).

The *Token.* Boston: Goodrich, 1829.

The *Weekly Mirror,* 1844-1846 (edited with George P. Morris).

SECONDARY SOURCES

AUSER, CORTLAND P. "The Contribution of George P. Morris to American Journalism." Unpublished doctoral dissertation, New York University, 1960. Discussion of Willis' role in co-editorship.

BEERS, HENRY E. *Nathaniel Parker Willis.* Boston: Houghton, Mifflin, 1885. First full-length biography, now incomplete but valuable for quotations from letters no longer extant.

BROOKS, VAN WYCK. *The World of Washington Irving.* New York: E. P. Dutton, 1944. Brief reference to Willis comparing work to that of Irving and James.

CLARK, T. COTTRELL. "The Late N. P. Willis and Literary Men Forty Years Ago," *Northern Monthly,* II (November 1867-April, 1868), 235-37. Brief discussion of the Poe-Willis relationship.

DAUGHRITY, KENNETH L. "The Life and Work of Nathaniel P. Willis, 1806-1836." Unpublished doctoral dissertation, University of Virginia, 1935. Exhaustive and generally dependable work about early years.

————. "Poe's 'Quiz on Willis,'" *American Literature,* V (November, 1933), 55-62. Discussion of Poe's "Lionizing" as the "quiz."

HAYWOOD, EDWARD F. "Nathaniel Parker Willis," *Atlantic Monthly,* LIV (1884), 212-21. Brief survey of Willis' contribution to the writing of "polite literature."

HOLMES, OLIVER WENDELL. "Introduction," *A Mortal Antipathy.* Boston: Houghton, Mifflin, 1892. Impressionistic portrait of younger Willis.

HUGUENIN, CHARLES ARTHUR. "Nathaniel Parker Willis: His Literary Criticism of His Contemporaries." Unpublished doctoral dissertation, St. John's University, 1940. Detailed examination of Willis' critical statements.

LOWELL, JAMES RUSSELL. "A Fable for Critics," *The Poetical Works of James Russell Lowell.* Boston: Houghton, Mifflin, 1904. IV, 43-45.

PATTEE, FRED LEWIS. *The Development of the American Short Story.* New York, Harper and Brothers, 1923. Praises Willis' contribution in extended discussion, although sometimes unhistorical and inaccurate.

POE, EDGAR ALLAN. "N. P. Willis," in *Complete Works of Edgar Allan Poe*. New York: Putnams, 1902. VIII, 138-40; 226-44; 322-31. Review of magazine problems, "Tortesa the Usurer," as well as a balanced evaluation of Willis although not crediting him for intellect.

QUINN, ARTHUR H. *A History of the American Drama from the Beginning to the Civil War*. New York: Appleton-Century-Crofts, 1943. Sympathetic review of Willis' two successful plays in the native Romantic tradition.

————. *The Literature of the American People*. New York: Appleton-Century-Crofts, 1951. Sympathetic review of Willis' accomplishments with recommendation for re-examination of work.

RAUCH, BASIL. "The First Hundred Years," *Town and Country*, C (December, 1946), 60 ff. Review of Willis and Morris' accomplishments in establishing *Home Journal*, the immediate forerunner of *Town and Country*.

SCUDDER, HAROLD H. "Thackeray and N. P. Willis," *PMLA*, LVII (June, 1942), 589-92. Review of Willis' soliciting Thackeray for donations to the *Corsair*.

SPILLER, ROBERT E. *The American in England*. New York: Henry Holt and Company, 1926. Excellent and favorable account in detail of Willis' travel letters from England.

TAFT, KENNETH B. *Minor Knickerbockers*. New York: American Book Company, 1947. Detailed review of the times and the milieu in which Willis wrote; with short biography, detailed bibliography, and representative selections.

WEGELIN, CHRISTOF. *The Image of Europe in Henry James*. Dallas: Southern Methodist University Press, 1958. Discussion of Willis' European stories and his novel *Paul Fane;* recognition of Willis' early work in an area James was to work.

————. "The Rise of the International Novel," *PMLA*, LXXVII (June, 1962), 305-10. Article mainly on James's work but citing in detail the similarities between Willis' *Paul Fane* and James's work with respect to international society and manners.

Index

Index

Addison, Joseph, 26
Aldrich, Thomas B., 130
Alexander's Weekly Magazine, 56
Allen, Gay Wilson, 55, 115
Allston, Washington, 133
Almack's, 29, 141
American Monthly Magazine, 21, 25, 29
Atlantic Club Book, 118

Baillie, Joanna, 45, 112
Balzac, Honoré, 50, 120
Barrett, Elizabeth, 120
"Barry Cornwall," 43, 112, 120
Bartlett, W. H., 138
Beaumont, Francis, 26
Benjamin, Park, 29, 48, 50, 65 quoted
Bird, Robert Montgomery, 121
Blessington, Lady, 45, 47, 112
Boas, Ralph P., 120
"Boz," 50
Broadway Journal, 56
Brontë, Charlotte, 120
Brooks, Maria, 63
Browne, Sir Thomas, 26
Bryant, William Cullen, 27, 129
Bulwer-Lytton, Edward, 28, 29, 43, 50, 58, 112
Burton, Richard, 26
Butler, Pierce, 132
Byron, George Gordon Lord, 26, 40, 41, 82, 112, 119

Campbell, Thomas, 27, 45, 114
Cary sisters, 130
Cervantes, 26
Cheever, George B., 118
Child, Lydia Maria, 31, 63
"Christopher North," 24, 43, 54
Chubbock, Emily, 63; *see also* "Fanny Forester"
Cicero, 26
Civil War, 128-29
Clark, Lewis Gaylord, 46, 60

Clemm, Mrs., 58
Cole, Thomas, 39
Coleridge, Samuel T., 26, 116, 119
Cooper, James Fenimore, 27, 50
Cooper, Peter, 129
Copyright law, 62
Corsair, 48, 50
Cowper, William, 114
Cox, William, 50

Dana, Charles, 129
Dana, Richard Henry, 27
Dante, 26
Daughrity, Kenneth, 45
Defoe, Daniel, 26
Democratic Review, 60
Dibdin, Charles, 119
Dickens, Charles, 120; *see also* "Boz"
Disraeli, Benjamin, 27, 43, 112
Drake, Joseph Rodman, 129
Dryden, John, 26
Duganne, Augustus, 63
Duyckinck, Evert, 62
Dwight, Henry E., 34-35

Eliot, George, 68
Evening Post, 50
Everett, Edward, 128

"Fanny Fern," 130; *see also* Sara P. Willis
"Fanny Forester," 63; *see also* Emily Chubbock
Fay, Theodore, 50, 129
Fielding, Henry, 26
Ford, John, 26, 120
Forrest, Edwin, 132
Fuller, Frances A., 130
Fuller, Hiram, 55, 65

Gautier, Théophile, 120
Godey's, 63
Goethe, 120
Goodrich, Samuel P., 21, 22

"Grace Greenwood," 130
Graham's, 58, 63
Gray, Thomas, 115
Greeley, Horace, 48, 50
Greenough, Horatio, 39, 133
Griswold, Rufus, 58
Guiciolli, Countess, 38, 42

Hall, Basil, 27
Halleck, Fitz-Greene, 27, 129
Hawthorne, Nathaniel, 132
Hayne, Paul Hamilton, 130
Hazlitt, William, 120
Hemans, Felicia D., 27, 119
Heywood, Thomas, 26, 121
Hoffman, Charles F., 129
Holmes, Oliver Wendell, 130
Holton, Sarah T., 130
Hood, Thomas, 119
Horace, 27
Howe, Julia Ward, 130
Hunt, Leigh, 120

International novel, 27, 101-5
Irving, Washington, 27, 59, 66-67,
  69, 129, 143-44

James, Henry, 101, 104, 105
Jonson, Ben, 26
Juvenal, 27

Keats, John, 26
Kemble, Fanny, 132
Kettell, Samuel, 118
Kirkland, Caroline M., 130
Kock, Paul de, 120
Korner, Theodore, 120
Knickerbocker Magazine, 50, 60
Knickerbockerism, 129

La Fontaine, 120
Lamartine, Alphonse de, 120
Lamb, Charles, 27, 28, 43
Landon, Letitia E., 48
Landor, Walter Savage, 27, 112
Legendary, 21
Leggett, William, 27
Leonard, William Ellery, 111
Lind, Jenny, 132

Lockhart, John Gibson, 46
Longfellow, Henry Wadsworth, 19,
  63, 131
Lowell, James Russell, 114
Lynch, Anne, 62, 130

MacPherson, James, 26
MacReady riots, 132
Marlowe, Christopher, 26
Marryat, Frederick, 46
Martineau, Harriet, 120
Mellen, Grenville, 22
Melville, Herman, 62, 131
Merimée, Prosper, 120
Milton, John, 26
Mitford, Mary R., 120
Moore, Thomas, 43, 47, 112
Morris, George P., 19, 31, 32, 36,
  48, 51, 57, 81, 118
Morse, Samuel, 38
Mount, William, 132
Mowatt, Anna Cora, 63
Musset, Alfred de, 120

National Press, 55
Natural aristocracy, 96-100
Neal, John, 22
New Mirror, 54, 55
New Monthly Magazine, 22
New World, 119
North American Review, 50

O'Brien, Fitz-James, 130
Osgood, Frances S., 63, 130

Parton, James, 131
Pattee, Fred Lewis, 26, 68
Paulding, James K., 27
Percival, Emily, 57
Poe, Edgar Allan, *see* Willis
Pope, Alexander, 26, 112
Porter, Jane, 45, 115
Porter, T. O., 48, 50
Praed, Winthrop T., 45

Raleigh, Sir Walter, 26
Ray, Gordon, 49
Read, Thomas B., 130
Richter, Jean Paul, 120

Rives, William Cabell, 37
Rogers, Samuel, 27, 45, 114

Sand, George, 120
Schiller, Friedrich, 120
Scott, Sir Walter, 27
Scribe, Eugène, 120
Scudder, Harold H., 49
Sedgwick, Catherine, 27
Shelley, Percy Bysshe, 26
Snelling, William, 31
Spiller, Robert, 42 quoted
Sprague, Charles, 27, 130
Sterne, Laurence, 26
Stoddard, Richard H., 130
Swift, Jonathan, 26

Taft, Kendall B., 68, 118
Tatler, 59
Taylor, Bayard, 45, 130
Taylor, Jeremy, 26, 27
Thackeray, William M., 49, 120
Thomson, James, 114
Thorwaldson, Albert, 39
Tieck, Ludwig, 120
Timrod, Henry, 130
Token, 21, 22

Virgil, 27
Verplanck, Gulian, 129
Virtue, George, 138

Webster, John, 26
Wegelin, Christof, 105, 146-47
Wetmore, Prosper M., 129
Whitman, Sarah Helen, 57
Whitman, Walt, 55
Whittier, John G., 132
Willis, Nathaniel P., anthologist, 118-19; associations with Edgar Allan Poe, 28, 29, 38, 45, 55, 56-60, 124; attacks on, 46-47; comments on British society, 40, 42, 47, 90; critical evaluation of, 28-30; early life, 19-21; editorship of *American Monthly Magazine*, 22-26; *Corsair*, 48-49; *Evening Mirror*, 55, 60, 61; *Home Journal*, 58, 125-34, 148; *New Mirror*, 54-55, 58; *New York Mirror*, 31-33, 47, 50-53; *Weekly Mirror*, 63; education, 20; evaluation of contributions, 146-49; humor, 94-95; international novel, 101-5; natural nobility, 96-100; newspaper experience, 64-65; plays, 120-24; profession of taste, 148-49; prose writer, evaluation as, 144-45; reading and literary influences, 26-27; romances, 76-89; sketcher, as, 69, 78; story teller, evaluation as, 105-7; travels: in England, 43, 135-37; in Europe, 40, 42, 49; in Italy, Florence, and Rome, 36, 38-40; in France and Paris, 37-38; in Near East, 40-41; in United States, 70, 71, 137-38, 140-41; in West Indies, 139-40

WRITINGS OF:

Poems and poetic volumes:
"Absalom," 109, 113
"The Belfrey Pigeon," 28, 78
"Better Moments," 116
"Birthday Verses," 117
"The Confessional," 111
"Contemplations," 116
"To a Coquette," 117
"Dawn," 116
"Despondency in Spring," 111
"The Dying Alchymist," 28, 109
"To Ermengarde," 116
"Fail Me Not Thou," 111
"Florence Gray," 111, 112
Fugitive Pieces, 109
"Hagar in the Wilderness," 113
"To the Lady in the Chemisette," 117
"Lady Jane," 112
"The Leper," 109, 113
"Lines on Leaving Europe," 117
"Lord Ivan and his Daughter," 121
Melanie and Other Poems, 109
"Misanthropic Musings," 111
"To My Mother from the Apennines," 117

"Parrhasius," 109
Poems of Passion, 109
Poems, Sacred, Passionate, and Humorous, 109
"Refreshing Retrospections," 115
"Reverie at Glenmary," 115
"Roaring Brook," 116
Sacred Poems, 109
"Sacrifice of Abraham," 113
"Saturday Afternoon," 116
"Saul," 28, 113
"The Scholar of Thebat ben Chorat," 28, 109
"She Was Not There," 111
"The Shumanite," 113
Sketches, 109
"Thirty-five," 117
"Thought While Making the Grave of a New Born Child," 116
"Waking Dream in Sickness," 116
"The White Chip Hat," 117
"The Wife's Appeal," 28, 109

Prose writings:

"Albina McLush," 74
"The Alias—or Mr. St. John," 74
"The Bandit of Austria," 86
"Baron Von Raffleoff," 27, 73
"The Belle of the Belfrey," 87
"Beauty and the Beast," 99
Bianca Visconti (play), 108, 121-23
"Born to Have Pigs and Chickens," 98
"Brown's Day at the Mimpson's," 99
"Captain Thompson," 27, 74
"The Cherokee's Threat," 96
"Confessions of a Disliked Man," 72
The Convalescent, 135, 143
"Count Pott's Strategy," 91
"Countess Nyschreim and the Handsome Artist," 86
"Death of the Gentle Usher," 71
"The Disturbed Vigil," 77

"Driving Stanhope Pro Tem," 74, 75
"Edith Linsey," 76, 77
"The Elopement," 73, 74
"The Exile," 28, 72
Famous Persons and Places, 135
"The Fancy Ball," 27, 73, 74
"The Female Ward," 94
"Frost and Flirtation," 78
"F. Smith," 45, 79, 88
"The Ghost Ball at Congress Hall," 90
"The Gypsy of Sardis," 45, 82
Health Trip to the Tropics, 135, 139, 140
Hurrygraphs, 135, 138, 141
"The Icy Veil," 94
"Incidents on the Hudson," 45, 79, 80
"Incidents in the Life of a Quiet Man," 71
Inklings of Adventure, 70, 83
"The Inlet of Peach Blossoms," 87, 88
"Kate Crediford," 94
"Lady Rachel," 92
"Lady Ravelgold's Romance," 91
"Larks on Vacation," 45, 79
"The Last Bachelor," 28, 74
"Leaves from a Colleger's Album," 21, 69
"Leaves from the Heart-Book of Ernest Clay," 92-93
"Lecture on Fashion," 119
"Letters of Horace Fritz," 27, 69
"Letters from Under a Bridge," 119, 135, 142-43
"Light Vervain," 100
"A Log in the Archipelago," 135
Loiterings of Travel, 136-37
"Love and Diplomacy," 45, 88
"Love and Speculation," 78
"Love in the Library," 45
"The Lunatic's Skate," 77
"Mabel Wynne," 98
"The Madhouse at Palermo," 45, 83
"The Mad Suitor," 77

"The Marquis in Petticoats," 87
"Meena Dimity," 98, 99
"Minute Philosophies," 70, 78, 80
"Miss Jones' Son," 100
"A Morning in the Library," 71, 76
"Mrs. Passable Trott," 94
"My One Adventure as a Brigand," 86
"New Series of Letters from London," 47
"Niagara," 79
"Nora Mehidy," 95
"Notes upon a Ramble," 27, 70-71
Outdoors at Idlewild, 135
"Oonder-Hoofden," 81
"Paletto's Bride," 85
"Pasquali, the Tailor of Venice," 84
"Passages from an Epistolary Journal," 137
Paul Fane, 101-5
"P. Calamus," 75
"Pedlar Karl," 45, 76
Pencillings by the Way, 27, 34-42
People I Have Met, 68
"The Phantom Head upon the Table," 87
"The Picker and the Piler," 81
"The Poet and the Mandarin," 87, 88

"A Revelation of a Private Life," 87
"The Revenge of Signor Basil," 84
Rural Letters, 68, 110, 138-39
"The Ruse," 22, 69
"St. Lawrence," 79
"Scenes of Fear," 45, 76
"The Scrapbook," 71
"The Spirit Love of 'Ione S.'," 95-96
"Tête à Tête Confessions," 25, 71
"Tom Fane and I," 79, 80
Tortesa, 23-24, 108
"Two Buckets in a Well," 98
"Unwritten Music," 70
"Unwritten Philosophy," 21
"Unwritten Poetry," 21
"An Uptown Crisis," 90
"Widow by Brevet," 82
"The Wife Bequeathed and Rescued," 87, 88
"Wigwam vs. Almack's," 97
"Winter Scene in New England," 71, 78
Willis, Sara P. ("Fanny Fern"), 130
Winter, William, 130
Woodworth, Samuel, 32, 129
Wordsworth, William, 26, 80, 115

Yale, 20
"Young America," 62